AMERICAN HERITAGE

April, 1970 · Volume XXI, Number 3

Our issue this month is full of venerable institutions, if we may use both those words rather broadly; and the things that have happened to them, taking the long view, are fine examples of what makes history so endlessly fascinating. Several institutions are changed almost beyond recognition, like the three-hundred-year-old Hudson's Bay Company, whose dramatic tale we tell on the following pages. Or they have a new "image," like the philosophical squire of Topeka, Alf M. Landon, interviewed on page 93 in his eighty-third year. Some institutions that might have been thought certain to endure for centuries, such as the Amoskeag mills (page 110) and the Everglades (page 97), are in dire peril, while others look very much the same, like Jay Gould's mansion, Lyndhurst (page 46), where the table is still set for a dinner that seems to be indefinitely postponed.

Another institution that looks much the same, albeit refurbished on the outside, is the Metropolitan Museum of Art in New York.

The picture above was taken there some sixty years ago, when art was representational and old-fashioned patriotism was very popular. The demure little group are inspecting Emanuel Leutze's heroic canvas Washington Crossing the Delaware. That picture was later relegated to the basement and finally went out of the collection altogether on permanent loan to a smaller museum near the site of the event portrayed. This month the Metropolitan celebrates its hundredth anniversary, but the scene behind the unchanging façade is rather different. The little mod group below is looking at Robert Motherwell's Elegy to the Spanish Republic; the picture speaks its own proverbial thousand words about the fate of art and old-fashioned patriotism without any further help from us. We must confine ourselves to wishing all these institutions well and to suggesting that another picture taken in the same place some ten or twenty years hence will be just as surprising, and that the only thing certain is change itself.

AMERICAN HERITAGE

The Magazine of History

SENIOR EDITOR
Bruce Catton

EDITOR
Oliver Jensen

MANAGING EDITOR
Robert Lincoln Reynolds

ARTICLES EDITOR
E. M. Halliday

PICTURE EDITOR
Douglas Tunstell

ASSOCIATE EDITOR
Barbara Klaw

ART DIRECTOR
Chester Prosinski

COPY EDITOR: Carol Angell

ASSISTANT EDITORS
Carla Davidson   Mary Dawn Earley
Mary A. H. Sachs

CONSULTING EDITOR: Joan Paterson Kerr

CONSERVATION EDITOR
David G. McCullough

ASSOCIATE CONSERVATION EDITOR
Elizabeth N. Layne

PUBLISHER: Paul Gottlieb

ADVISORY BOARD
Allan Nevins, *Chairman*

Carl Carmer   Louis C. Jones
Gerald Carson   Alvin M. Josephy, Jr.
Marshall B. Davidson   Howard H. Peckham
John A. Garraty   Francis S. Ronalds
Eric F. Goldman   S. K. Stevens

American Heritage Publishing Co., Inc.

PRESIDENT
James Parton

CHAIRMAN, EDITORIAL COMMITTEE
Joseph J. Thorndike

MANAGING DIRECTOR, BOOK DIVISION
Richard M. Ketchum

EDITORIAL ART DIRECTOR
Murray Belsky

AMERICAN HERITAGE is published every two months by American Heritage Publishing Co., Inc.; editorial and executive offices, 551 Fifth Avenue, New York, N.Y. 10017. Treasurer, George W. Breitkreuz; Secretary, John C. Taylor III. Correspondence about subscriptions should be sent to American Heritage Subscription Office, 383 West Center Street, Marion, Ohio 43302. Single copies: $5.00. Annual subscriptions: $20.00 in U.S. and Canada; $21.00 elsewhere. An annual Index is published each spring, priced at $1.00. AMERICAN HERITAGE will consider but assumes no responsibility for unsolicited materials. Title registered U.S. Patent Office. Second-class postage paid at New York, N.Y., and at additional mailing offices.

Sponsored by
American Association for State & Local History · Society of American Historians

CONTENTS *April, 1970 · Volume XXI, Number 3*

COVER: This spring marks the three-hundredth anniversary of North America's most venerable commercial enterprise, The Governor and Company of Adventurers of England Trading Into Hudson's Bay—known more simply as the Hudson's Bay Company or, in twentieth-century shorthand, "the Bay." This painting is by Frances Anne Hopkins, who as the wife of the private secretary to one of the company's great governors, Sir George Simpson, often went along on inspection trips. Here they are, seated amidships, with Mrs. Hopkins' head just visible between two burly paddlers. As befits a proper Victorian lady, her hat is firmly on her head, and she seems supremely confident that the canoe, like the company and the Empire itself, will triumphantly survive all perils. An article marking the Bay's tricentennial begins on page 4. *Back Cover:* The isolated existence of the polar bear is no longer as serene as in this painting; indeed, the animal may be facing total extinction. The details are in this month's Field Notes on page 117. C.S. Raleigh's painting is in the Edgar William and Bernice Chrysler Garbisch Collection at the National Gallery of Art.

Still doing business at the old stand . . .

HUDSON'S BAY ASSETS

1670	1970
1 leaky ketch	2 large ships
	4 barges
1 abandoned canoe	3 tugs
	3 airplanes
2 or 3 pairs of used snowshoes	575 trucks
	God knows how many snowmobiles
1 naturally air-conditioned log hut	8 large air-conditioned department stores
	25 medium-sized department stores
1 small load of beaver pelts, partially exchanged for baubles, bangles, and brandy	217 smaller stores
	3 of the world's largest fur auctions
	65 million dollars' worth of merchandise on hand, including an ample supply of Hudson's Bay Scotch Whisky
14 employees	15,000 employees, give or take a few
38.8% of Canada	.0017% of Canada

Having worked like a beaver to overcome three
centuries of plunging thermometers, recalcitrant Indians, and
fierce competitors from Quebec and the U.S.A., it
remains today the continent's most durable trading enterprise

The Hudson's Bay Company

By DAVID LAVENDER
With drawings by RONALD SEARLE

During the centuries-long expansion of the Hudson's Bay Company throughout Canada, its initials, emblazoned on the flags it flew, became ubiquitous. There were even jokes about the symbols. HBC —What did that stand for? asked the tenderfoot. And the old trapper took another pull at his clay pipe before replying gravely, "Here Before Christ."

More literally, the firm—its official name was "The Governor and Company of Adventurers of England Trading into Hudson's Bay"—was granted its charter by Charles II of England three hundred years ago, on May 2, 1670. Straightway it was beset by such

troubles that during its first forty-eight years it paid only four dividends to its stockholders. Although profits became steadier thereafter, it remained subject to violent attacks from opponents in the field and to scathing denunciations in Parliament. Yet always it triumphed, rich, venerable, and prestigious—the Honourable Company, as its friends sometimes described it, in simple majesty.

Doggedness rather than zest was the key. The company's traders were still groping for the techniques that would let them survive in the windswept muskeg beside their frozen bay when they were challenged by French winterers

5

from the St. Lawrence—audacious men thoroughly familiar with the cascading waterways that furnished the only trade routes through the armadillo shell of granite that covers most of eastern Canada. Unable to outmaneuver this formidable enemy, the English sat tight until at last war and international diplomacy eliminated France entirely from the New World.

There was no surcease beside the bay, however. The famed North West Company, a belligerent union of Highland Scotsmen and American colonists,

Groseilliers and Radisson with Prince Rupert

stepped into the shoes of the French and resumed a trade war that soon spread across the Rockies to the Pacific. But the Honourable Company outlasted their furious energy, too, and took over the entire northland. With two centuries of such experience fortifying them, the new overlords of the wilderness had little trouble turning back a brief challenge from American trappers in the Pacific Northwest. Settlers, however, were something else. They could outstay even the Honourable Company. With unfailing resilience the traders turned to serving the newcomers rather than fighting them. So the flag with its ubiquitous initials stayed aloft, as familiar now as breathing to thousands of people who never heard of the old, dashing enemies from Montreal.

Curiously enough, the inevitabilities of geography that let the English acquire their first stubborn foothold in Canada

were first appreciated by two outlawed French traders. And they reached their conclusions without even laying eyes on the vast bay that was the key to the situation.

The elder and leader of the pair was Médart Chouart, Sieur des Groseilliers. The other, his brother-in-law, was Pierre Esprit Radisson.

Groseilliers came to Canada from France as a youth about 1640, when prospects in the little settlements along the St. Lawrence River were bleak. The fur trade, the only business of consequence in the colony, was dominated by a legally created monopoly that held its favored position by financing the government. All independent trading in furs was forbidden.

In an effort to make the interdiction effective, the monopolists sought to confine the trade to a handful of rendezvous points scattered along the St. Lawrence River. Each year hundreds of Indians came to these sites in fleets of fur-laden canoes. They picked up cloth, iron tools, guns, and ammunition from the legally licensed traders and carried the articles back into the wilderness. There they traded the goods to more distant tribes. Since the role of middleman was profitable, rivalries developed among the Indians. By seizing control of the rugged transportation routes that led from the French settlements to the upper Great Lakes, the Huron tribes became dominant.

Meanwhile Dutch and English traders were pressing northward along the Hudson River. They, too, worked through Indian middlemen—the confederated tribes that made up the Iroquois nation. When the Iroquois sought to handle pelts that otherwise would have been traded by the Huron, explosive wars broke out.

The whites joined the rivalry. They armed their Indians and provided them with early-day technical advisers—bold young men who lived with the tribes, cajoled them into resisting the blandishments of the other side, and helped them in their battles. Associated with the emissaries from the St. Lawrence were Jesuit priests, who joined the trading groups in order to live with the heathens they hoped to convert.

In 1646 young Médart Chouart (he had not yet become Sieur des Groseilliers) travelled with a group of Jesuits to

Huronia, on the shores of Georgian Bay, the northeastern bulge of rock-bound Lake Huron. He learned firsthand the staggering difficulties of toiling in a canoe up the Ottawa and Mattawa rivers, of portaging around the rapids while black flies and mosquitoes devoured him, and of slogging through fetid marshes in order to cross the low divide near Lake Nipissing. He learned, too, that the Huron were starting their long slide into defeat. In 1648 and again in 1649 Iroquois raiders swept through the Huronia villages, killing and ravaging. The shattered Huron fled west to new homes around Lake Michigan and south of Lake Superior.

The dispersal left the French settlements in desperate straits. The trade on which they depended had ceased to exist. In 1652 not one beaver pelt reached the warehouses at Montreal.

The next year hope revived. Via roundabout northern routes three canoes slipped into the village of Trois Rivières, below Montreal, with reports that a new Indian trading fair was being organized far to the west. Simultaneously an Iroquois delegation approached Quebec with an offer of peace.

Groseilliers undertook to find the new Huron villages and persuade the Indians that it was again safe to bring furs to the St. Lawrence. With a companion he spent the winter of 1654–55 at Green Bay, a western arm of Lake Michigan. The next summer, while prowling through what is now northern Wisconsin to spread the good news, the two men picked up reports of an enormous wealth of unexploited beaver around Lake Superior. The following year they led a flotilla of richly laden canoes back over the long waterways from Lake Superior to the St. Lawrence.

Montreal rejoiced. Rewarded with a part of the furs, Groseilliers settled with his wife on a seigniory near Trois Rivières. There he took to swapping tales with Madame Groseilliers' half brother, Pierre Radisson.

Radisson's career had been equally strenuous. In 1651, aged fifteen, he had been captured by Mohawk and adopted by one of their families. For attempting to escape, he was bound in such a way that he could contemplate his own coming punishment by watching the torture of fellow captives. He witnessed the slow disembowelment of a pregnant Frenchwoman and the pouring of molten lead into the wounds of other victims. As for himself, he wrote later, a Mohawk warrior "run through my foot a swoord red out of the fire and plucked several of my nails." But, he added, his foster parents intervened to keep things from growing really rough.

As soon as he could walk, he made another break, reached the Dutch in upper New York, and returned to Canada by way of France. Shortly thereafter he joined a mission that the Jesuits were preparing to send among the Onondaga

in response to the Iroquois peace feeler of 1653. He traded on the side, and when he returned to Trois Rivières in 1657, still only twenty-one, he was a seasoned veteran.

Fired by their own talk, Groseilliers and Radisson decided to tap the fur supply of the Lake Superior region. When they applied to Governor d'Argenson for licenses, he imposed conditions that would have made him a secret, nonworking partner in the venture. Unwilling to pay so high a price, the brothers-in-law impulsively decamped overnight with a group of westbound Indians, confident that if they achieved a success like

Groseilliers' in 1656 their illegality would be forgiven.

They survived a starving winter at Chequamegon Bay, on the southwestern shore of Lake Superior. When the ice broke in the spring of 1660, they chanced to meet a party of wild, shy Cree Indians from the north. These Cree had with them, for trade to Huron or Ottawa middlemen, the glossiest beaver pelts that the French traders had ever seen. Eagerly the two entrepreneurs inquired about the source of the furs. As an incident to the answers, they heard of massive rivers that rose beyond a nearby divide of ice-scoured granite (the high

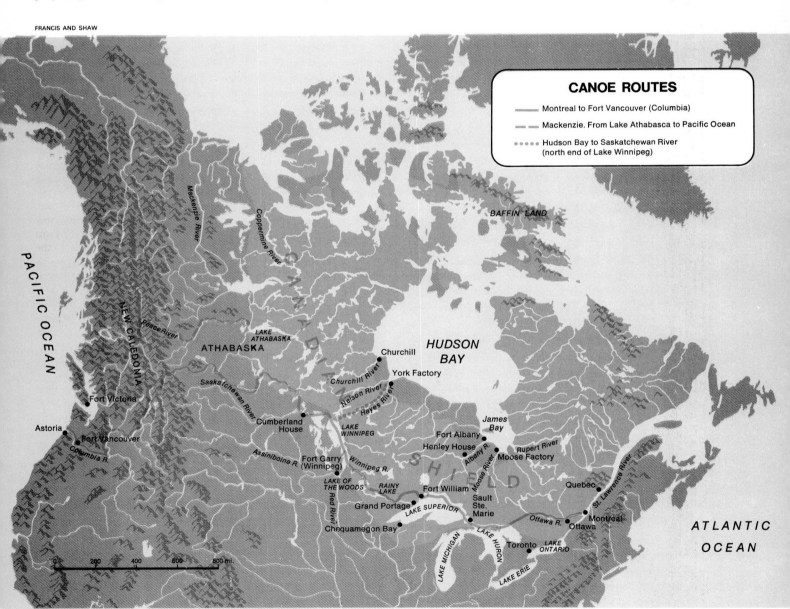

part of the Canadian Shield) and ran northward to an inland sea of salt water. The journey to that sea, the Cree went on, was neither long nor laborious.

The implications were startling, for the foaming waterways that the Frenchmen had followed through the Shield from Montreal were both long and extraordinarily difficult. Now it seemed that there might be an easier way.

One can imagine them scratching lines into the earth with twigs so as to bring into focus such geography as they knew. Though ill-informed about early sea explorations to the north, they somehow guessed, wildly but accurately, that the Cree salt water was Hudson Bay. Speculation leaped. Would the government finance them on a scouting trip to learn whether it was possible for a ship to creep into the bay at the beginning of each brief summer, lure the Indians to a trading rendezvous at the mouth of one of the rivers, and then leave with the furs before the ice closed in? If developments were favorable, would they be granted a monopoly?

True, they were currently operating outside the law. In view of the circumstances, however, their small dereliction about licenses surely would be overlooked.

Hopefully they returned to trade-starved Montreal at the head of a fleet of Indian canoes "that did almost cover ye whole river." But the axe fell anyway. After imposing the normal 25 per cent tax on the portion of furs that Groseilliers and Radisson considered their own, Governor d'Argenson added fines that were all but confiscatory, and pocketed the bulk of the proceeds for himself. He also declined to hear talk of a route through Hudson Bay. Why should he listen? Opening a rival path to the interior would dilute the monopoly of the St. Lawrence.

Outraged, Groseilliers hurried to Paris to protest the fines and to ask for help in reaching Hudson Bay. He was brushed aside. But the thought of those wonderful furs kept the brothers-in-law from admitting defeat. Twice they hired ships in the hope of reaching the bay on their own, and twice they failed. Persisting still, they went to England. There, after long delays occasioned by outbreaks of plague, war, and London's great fire, they gained audiences both with King

Charles II and with the King's cousin Prince Rupert. After more delays the prince eventually assembled half a dozen or so men who were willing to underwrite the explorations the Frenchmen proposed.

Two diminutive ships were loaded with trade goods—the *Eaglet*, forty feet long, of fifty-four tons burden, and the *Nonsuch*, a ketch thirty-seven feet long and of forty tons burden. Although Radisson and Groseilliers supervised most of the preparatory details, they were not allowed to take charge of the expedition. They were Frenchmen. In case of war between France and England, there might be problems of loyalty. Furthermore, if the adventure did result in notable discoveries, there would be protection for England in having it done under the aegis of a British citizen. Command, therefore, was given to Zachariah Gillam of Boston, Massachusetts, an experienced seaman who was also captain of the *Nonsuch*. Radisson and Groseilliers—whom the English insisted on calling Mr. Gooseberry—would go along as consultants.

The two ships sailed from Gravesend, on the Thames, on June 3, 1668. In mid-Atlantic a storm engulfed them. The *Eaglet*, with Radisson aboard, was damaged so severely that she had to turn back. The *Nonsuch*, on which Groseilliers had sailed, continued through Hudson Strait and turned along the flat eastern shore to the nipple at the southern end, James Bay.

Gillam beached the *Nonsuch* inside the mouth of a river that he named the Rupert. Close beside the ship the crew built Fort Charles, a hut of logs erected picket style. Though they lived well enough on wild fowl and fish, they were appalled by the six months of almost unimaginable cold.

News of their presence spread from Indian to Indian. Hundreds appeared at the spring thaw to exchange beaver pelts for the inestimable boon of tools, metal cooking utensils, cloth, and bright, cheap jewelry. Obviously trade could succeed in the bay. Delighted with the prospects they had opened, the adventurers hurried back to London, arriving October 9, 1669.

The lush furs caused a sensation. During the ensuing winter Prince Rupert

easily persuaded eighteen men (he and the original backers included) to invest an average of three hundred pounds each toward forming a company for developing the trade. On May 2, 1670, King Charles granted this group a royal charter authorizing it to carry on commerce in "Furrs, Mineralls and other considerable commodityes." On parchment, at least, H.B.C. had come into existence.

The charter also granted the company title to the entire watershed of Hudson Bay. In time surveyors would calculate the area at 1,486,000 square miles, or ten times the extent of England, Wales, Scotland, and Ireland combined. The document then went on to describe the legal mechanics whereby colonies, or "plantations," complete with administrative officials and law courts, could be established in the area.

All this was a gambit in international chess-playing. In 1670 not Charles II, Groseilliers, Gillam, or anyone else could have had the least notion about the extent of the territory involved. Amounts did not matter. The real purpose was to counter in advance any conflicting claims that France might try to assert on the plea that her citizens had settled Canada first. By declaring an intention to plant a colony where no Frenchman (except Groseilliers) had yet set foot, the English might be able to contain their rivals within the granite-cramped bounds of the St. Lawrence.

Management of the new company was placed in the hands of a governor (Prince Rupert was the first) and a committee of seven. Although they were called "Adventurers Trading into Hudson's Bay," none of the English shareholders had the least intention of risking either the icebergs or the Indians. Supervision of that work was entrusted to a resident director, also called governor. The first one was Charles Bayly, a dour Quaker who had played with King Charles as a lad but had later been clapped into the Tower of London for his all but seditious criticism of the lax ways of the court. Bayly evidently considered exile at Hudson Bay preferable to confinement in the Tower, and Charles obliged him by foisting him off onto the Honourable Company.

Aided primarily by Radisson and Groseilliers, Bayly soon established three posts on the southern perimeter of James

*Above: Indians collecting furs for H.B.C.; be-
low: gloom in London, 1691–1717: no dividend*

Bay: Fort Charles, enlarged with brick
and mortar; Moose Factory at the mouth
of Moose River; and north of Moose
Factory, Fort Albany. Because each post
offered better blankets, hardware, and
guns than did the French traders from
Montreal, Indians flocked to them. The
Cree, who lived to the south, and the
Assiniboin, who lived to the southwest,
began jockeying for position as middlemen. Abruptly the French awoke to the

realization that thousands of pelts that
once would have worked their way
through aboriginal trade routes to the
St. Lawrence were now being diverted
to the Bay.

The officials in Quebec were in a
quandary. Choice northern beaver skins,
as contrasted with poorer pelts from
farther south, were still the lifeblood of
the colony's economy. The English traders *had* to be checked—but, unhappily,
France and England were currently
yoked together as uneasy allies against
the Dutch. Fearing that an overt attack
on the posts at the bay would bring
thunder from Paris, the unhappy men at
Quebec decided to tiptoe around the
dilemma.

One move was to assemble representatives of fifteen Indian tribes at a great
council beside the roaring cataracts—
the Sault—of St. Mary's River, the link
between Lake Huron and Lake Superior.
There, on June 4, 1671, with the assent
of the Indians, who hardly understood
what was happening, a bewigged and
bespangled representative of the King of
France proclaimed French sovereignty
over all the lands roundabout, as far as
the western, northern, and southern seas.
Mere words, of course—but to French
minds as good as the words in the charter
of the Hudson's Bay Company.

In marked contrast to this pomp were
two spying missions undertaken for
Montreal by a remarkable Jesuit, Father
Albanel, who travelled to the bay by foot
and canoe with small parties of Indians.
On his second trip, in 1674, Albanel
struck Governor Bayly as being altogether too friendly with Groseilliers, who
was wintering there. In the spring Bayly
sent the pair under suspicion to London, where the embarrassed committee
quickly apologized. This was not enough
for Radisson and Groseilliers, however. They felt underpaid at best. Their
brains had been well picked, and as
the need for their advice had declined,
they had found themselves treated with
increasing disdain. Aroused by this last
indignity, they followed Albanel to
France and there sought to interest the
French court in backing a competitive
invasion of the bay.

Paris declined to respond. Years passed
before the brothers-in-law made contact
with a wealthy merchant of Quebec,
Charles Aubert de la Chesnaye, who, in

spite of frowns from the governor, had
been trying to set into motion exactly the
sort of enterprise that Radisson and
Groseilliers were proposing. He was delighted to obtain their know-how.

Loading two small ships with goods,
the trio sailed in 1682 from Quebec to a
low, marshy point of land between the
Hayes and Nelson rivers, on the western
shore of the great bay. To their astonish-
ment two other parties appeared almost
at once. The first was a group of Bos-
tonians led by Benjamin Gillam, son of
Zachariah Gillam of the Hudson's Bay
Company. Shortly thereafter along came
Zachariah himself, in charge of the
company ship *Rupert*. With Gillam was a
new resident governor, John Bridgar, big
with plans for building a factory at the
point.

There were many Indians about, and
during the winter the rival groups did
not dare weaken themselves with quar-
rels. As it was, there were casualties
enough. Winds swept the *Rupert* out to
sea, where she was crushed by ice. In the
disaster Zachariah Gillam and several
hands perished.

At the first sign of spring, while the
others were off guard, Chesnaye, Radisson, and Groseilliers pounced. They
made prisoners of everyone. After con-
structing one sound ship of their two
winter-battered craft, they loaded aboard
it all the men of the Hudson's Bay Company except Governor Bridgar and sent
them to the posts at James Bay. Smugly
the Frenchmen then appropriated the
New England ship, the *Batchellor's Delight*, and both parties' furs for themselves. Leaving Groseilliers' son in charge
of Port Nelson, as they called their post,
they sailed to Quebec, taking the New
Englanders and Governor Bridgar along
as prisoners.

The governor in Quebec promptly released the captives and restored their
ship to them. In spite of the conciliatory
gesture, the Hudson's Bay Company
charged piracy, asked heavy damages,
and sought to use the incident as a means
of obtaining French recognition of their
claims to the entire watershed of Hudson
Bay. Although the French government
refused the demands, it did disavow the
action of the traders and ordered them
to apologize.

At some point during the dispute
Groseilliers died. On his own now, dis-

gusted by what he considered French abjectness, and influenced by his wife, who was the daughter of one of the Honourable Company's original shareholders, Radisson returned to English service. Sailing to the Nelson River in 1684, he captured from the French the fort he had built there and persuaded young Groseilliers also to switch allegiance to the Hudson's Bay Company. It was Radisson's last notable service for the firm he had helped originate.

That same year the company declared its first dividend, a thumping one of 50 per cent. Not all was well, however. The French were growing aggressive. Stung by Radisson's defection, mariners of the Quebec firm that once had employed him seized a Hudson's Bay Company ship in 1685 and carried it as a prize to the St. Lawrence. There a new governor greeted the raiders not with reprimands but with congratulations. The next year the same governor sent thirty soldiers and seventy *voyageurs* overland to James Bay. Surprise was total— and, anyway, the English cannon pointed toward the sea. The French captured the three southern posts. Only Port Nelson remained in English hands.

At first the losses caused surprisingly little hurt. The Nelson River, more than the streams of James Bay, tapped the heartland of the north, and Indians flocked down it with their furs. In 1690, flushed with euphoria, the London directors voted a three-for-one stock split and then declared a 25 per cent dividend on the augmented total.

The move was premature. At the bay trade had already slacked off. The persistent French had at last pushed through the granitic Shield into the heartland and were diverting part of its furs to the St. Lawrence.

The breakthrough was a triumph in environmental adaptation. Even as recently as the days of Groseilliers the colonial fur monopoly had continued to urge the Indians to sell their furs at controlled rendezvous sites along the St. Lawrence. As the white population grew, however, increasing numbers of unlicensed *coureurs de bois* took to breaking the pattern. They smuggled goods to distant Indian villages, picked up the furs on the spot, and smuggled the pelts back to illegitimate market places.

In an effort to meet this shadowy competition, the monopoly began sending its own traders among the Indians. A race began. Building on years of experience, the aggressive French learned how to take their birch-bark canoes westward to the region north of Lake Superior, near Lake Nipigon. They managed to arrive just as the Indians of the area were starting their trips to Port Nelson, soon rechristened York Factory. But why make the journey when the French were at hand? The Indians bartered as many of their finest pelts to the newcomers as the traders could handle in their canoes, and then let the surplus, mostly coarser, cheaper furs, go down the rivers to York.

The English reaction was stodgy but firm. The traders at Hudson Bay lacked the long experience with Indians that their rivals possessed. They were afraid of the vast, silent lands of the interior. Moreover, they could not find on those barren coasts the birch bark and cedar necessary for building canoes. In the face of these difficulties it would be better, the directors decided, not to compete in the interior but to step up efforts to bring more Indians to York Factory. After all, the English, too, had advantages. The quantity of merchandise that the French could carry over the long canoe routes from Montreal was limited. York Factory, by contrast, was stocked by ocean ship with an abundance of superior cloth, ironware, and tasty Brazilian tobacco. If a qualified emissary were sent among the Indians to urge these truths, the flow of trade would surely resume.

The messenger chosen for the promotional trip was Henry Kelsey, aged twenty. Kelsey had come to Port Nelson about the same time as Radisson, in 1684. He had accepted the new world with a boy's wide-eyed delight. Unlike most of his fellows, he preferred the nomadic camps of the Indians to the boredom of the more comfortable trading posts. Carefree journeys along the bleak shores of the bay soon brought him a reputation as a traveller, and when the matter of a selling trip among the Cree and Assiniboin arose, he actually wanted to go.

He wandered joyously for two years. He kept a record of sorts, partly in doggerel. ("In sixteen hundred and ninetyth year / I set forth as plainly may appear . . .") It is not possible to tell from his

meager descriptions exactly where he did go, but he certainly reached the Saskatchewan River, followed it westward a distance, and then turned south into the Great Plains, country that the French had not yet touched.

In 1692 he brought back to York Factory "a good fleet of Indians" and the first written description of the Canadian interior. Nothing came of it. During his absence France and England had declared war. Trade stagnated. Now and then warships of one nation or the other slid into the bay—the different posts changed hands repeatedly—and in 1697, during a climactic naval battle, Pierre Lemoyne, Sieur d'Iberville, sank a fifty-two-gun English man-of-war and captured one of the supply ships she was escorting. The price of Hudson's Bay Company stock crumbled from £260 to £80. For twenty-seven years, from 1691 through 1717, there were no dividends.

In Europe, English arms were more successful. The Treaty of Utrecht (1713) recognized the fact by confirming English sovereignty over the Hudson Bay drainage system and returning to the company the posts held by the French. The long work of rebuilding then began.

One new post, massive Fort Prince of Wales, was erected at the mouth of the Churchill River, far north of York Factory. The purpose was as conservative as ever—to lure in Indians, this time the Chipewyan, who lived around the icy shores of Great Slave Lake. Why do more? A postwar depression had slowed the French, and trade was dropping by default into English hands. Costs of less

TEXT CONTINUED ON PAGE 24

The Editors wish to thank the Hudson's Bay Company and its excellent quarterly, The Beaver, *for generous assistance in the preparation of the picture portfolio accompanying this article, and especially for permitting the use of the Ronald Searle drawings that illustrate the text. They are taken from* The Great Fur Opera, *by Kildare Dobbs, published next month under H.B.C. auspices. Incidentally, the American Association for State and Local History, one of the sponsors of the American Heritage Society and of this magazine, is presenting an Award of Merit to the Hudson's Bay Company in London on May 1, in recognition of its service to the historical profession in preserving three centuries' accumulation of company records.*

Here is the Nonsuch, *a ketch well named, plunging through North Atlantic waves in 1668 on her way to the founding of Canada's most famous business enterprise*

This painting, commissioned by the Honourable Company in anticipation of its three-hundredth anniversary celebration, makes a fit opening for a short but choice

Hudson's Bay Album

Governors and Adventurers

Prince Rupert, by Sir Peter Lely

James, Duke of York, by Jacob Huysmans

The Hudson's Bay Company was launched in an unsurmountably upper-crust ambiance, as indicated by the quality of its first three governors: Prince Rupert (who headed the company from 1670 to 1682); His Royal Highness, James, Duke of York, later King James II (1683–1685); and John Churchill, later the first Duke of Marlborough (1685–1692). Although all three were men of action who fought in the wars that beset their time, they viewed Hudson Bay primarily as an investment, and none of them ever made the slightest move to go and see the fabulous property. Rupert, who died in 1682, was chief author of the charter granted to the company in 1670; James's governorship was terminated when he mounted the throne; Churchill—who was to become one of England's great soldiers and ancestor of the late Prime Minister—lost the job when he intrigued with the exiled James in 1692.

John Churchill, by Sir Godfrey Kneller

Samuel Hearne's "A Winter View in the Athapuscow Lake" was drawn in 1771 at the western edge of what is now Manitoba.

The first century of the Hudson's Bay Company went meagerly recorded in pictures, for its employees were far better with axe and paddle than pen and brush. Samuel Hearne was an exception. In 1770–72 he was sent to explore the unknown country to the west and north; it was hoped that he might realize the long dream of a water passage connecting lower Hudson Bay with the Pacific. Hearne reached the disappointing but enlightening conclusion that no such passage existed. He also made some excellent sketches of the starkly beautiful country he traversed. Later he was placed in command of the company's most imposing structure, Fort Prince of Wales, which took thirty years to build and thirty minutes to surrender when three French warships surprised—or astonished—Hearne and his small garrison in 1782. (He had not heard of the war between England and France.) The French blew up the fort, but substantial ruins are still there.

Samuel Hearne, circa 1785

This engraving of "Prince of Wales's Fort," the proud Hudson's Bay bastion near Churchill, followed a 1777 Hearne drawing.

H.B.C.'s "Little Emperor"

Every great successful enterprise has a moving spirit, and if any one man is qualified for that title in the history of the Hudson's Bay Company, it is Sir George Simpson. Sent over from England as an understudy to the company's resident governor in 1820, young Simpson acquitted himself brilliantly in the fur-trade struggle with the North West Company. When the fierce competition ended in merger in 1821, he was clearly headed for the top. By 1826 he was governor-in-chief of H.B.C.'s vast territories; and that meant in effect ruling those territories as an agent of the British Crown. For almost forty years Simpson fulfilled his double task with the energy of a dynamo, driving the company to ever new heights of expansive efficiency. His organization of the great network of trappers, traders, factors, and commissioned officers has been compared both to that of the British Army and to that of the Catholic Church. He personally travelled nearly every mile of the H.B.C. trade routes, stopping overnight at all the important posts to confer with his officers in an atmosphere of businesslike conviviality. In the morning he would be up and away early, but not before a plunge in the icy water of the Saskatchewan River or Great Slave Lake, and not before a jaunty breakfast after that. Himself a bastard, he is said to have fathered numerous offspring by Indian concubines from the shores of Hudson Bay to the Pacific. He saw to it that these children were well cared for, meanwhile raising his proper family in a company mansion in a suburb of Montreal. Simpson was knighted by Queen Victoria in 1841. This was a recognition not only of his generally triumphant governorship of H.B.C. territories but also of his aid to British exploration parties in the Arctic and of his successful quasi-diplomatic negotiations with the Russians over British trade rights along the Canadian-Pacific coast and in the northwestern interior. He died in 1860, while H.B.C. still held its feudal proprietorship and trade monopoly of "Prince Rupert's Land" in undiminished splendor.

Cornelius Krieghoff's painting shows the first step in the fur trade: an H.B.C. agen

Michaelovski, a Russian fort and trading post near present-day Nome, Alaska, as it look

...egotiates with an Indian trapper for pelts.

...en painted by Frederick Whymper in 1867.

Governor Sir George Simpson

Argosies in Birch Bark

It has been said that the canoe would have made a good emblem for the Canadian coat of arms—so vital was the marvellous Indian birch-bark vessel in the exploration and development of the Canadian wilderness. The North West Company, which gave the Hudson's Bay Company its toughest commercial fight, depended on canoes of all sizes to get its men and their loads of fur through the otherwise impenetrable forests of the Canadian Shield. One of the canoe's chief merits was its light weight and hence its portability when it came to getting around dangerous rapids. Two ways of doing this are shown at

Even though Sir George Simpson dictated the use of York boats wherever possible to transport Hudson's Bay Company goods, he was fond of the canoe for his personal travel and for that of his officers. Eight experienced voyageurs *could move a big North canoe (like the one pictured above) through the water at a highly satisfactory clip, and keep going steadily for many hours. Always fond of pomp, Simpson enhanced the native majesty of his own canoe*

left (in a painting by an anonymous nineteenth-century artist) and at right (as seen by Cornelius Krieghoff in the 1850's). In its early years H.B.C. made relatively little use of canoes, instead encouraging the Indians to bring their furs to the shores of Hudson Bay for trading; later, as the company moved into the wilderness to set up posts, there was a tendency to favor the York boat, a double-prowed bateau twenty-eight to forty feet long that borrowed its qualities of shallow draft and maneuverability from the canoe but was much sturdier and capable of heavier loads. The canoe, nonetheless, never disappeared.

by bringing a Highland piper over from Scotland to sit behind him and pipe him in and out of important H.B.C. posts. His private secretary, Edward Martin Hopkins, often took along his wife, Frances Ann, who was an accomplished painter as well as an experienced canoe traveller. Here Mrs. Hopkins puts herself and her husband into the picture and the canoe in a superb painting done about 1870: Canoe Manned by Voyageurs.

H.B.C. and Oregon

A west-coast Indian custom was the potlatch (above), a feast at which a too lavish host often ruined himself. This one was at Fort Hope, B.C.

From 1825 to 1846 the Hudson's Bay Company in effect ruled all of what is now Oregon, Washington, and British Columbia. Two of its sturdy lieutenants there look out from these pages. Big John McLoughlin (above) established Fort Vancouver, now in Washington, as the company's far-west headquarters and ran it well from 1826 to 1846. When the lush region around today's Portland, Oregon, went to the United States after 1846, McLoughlin went too, quitting H.B.C. and becoming an American citizen there. He died an embittered old man in 1857, convinced that neither his old employer nor his new country had rightly appreciated him.

Fort George (below), on the Columbia River, was founded by John Jacob Astor as Astoria in 1811; it became McLoughlin's first far-west post.

James Douglas, McLoughlin's chief assistant for several years, explored Vancouver Island in the early 1840's, and as it looked likely that the United States would eventually possess the region south of the forty-ninth parallel *except* the tip of Vancouver, he superintended the building of Fort Victoria there. The island was made a British crown colony in 1849, and Douglas became its governor in 1851 while remaining chief H.B.C. officer in the west. He dealt firmly with inrushing American gold miners in 1858; and with the establishment of British Columbia that same year he finally left H.B.C. to become the new colony's governor.

Rugged Comforts of the Fur Trade

By 1900 even the more remote Hudson's Bay Company outposts offered solidly built houses and other amenities for employees. Here is Fort Simpson, in western British Columbia, in 1894. As the totem pole suggests, Indians were still around.

The York boat—named after its place of genesis, York Factory—was stable enough to permit a boating luxury: you could stand up to row. Here an H.B.C. crew maneuvers in easy fashion on the Saskatchewan in 1912.

It quite possibly was 40 degrees below zero outside, yet the Hudson's Bay Company factor and his wife had all the comforts of Toronto in their living room at a post somewhere along the Mackenzie River about 1900.

The Bay Today

GREENLAN

ALASKA

YUKON

Mackenzie River

DEVON ISLAND

BANKS
ISLAND

VICTORIA ISLAND

BAFFIN ISLAND

NORTHWEST   TERRITORIES

HUDSON BAY

BRITISH
COLUMBIA

Peace River

ALBERTA

Edmonton

SASKATCHEWAN

Churchill River

Nelson River

James
Bay

Q

PACIFIC

OCEAN

Victoria

Vancouver

Columbia River

Calgary

Saskatchewan River

Saskatoon

MANITOBA

ONTARIO

O

Regina

Winnipeg

LAKE SUPERIOR

LAKE HURON

To

LAKE
MICHIGAN

LAKE ERIE

UNITED STATES OF AMERICA

THE HUDSON'S BAY COMPANY TODAY

DEPARTMENT STORES
- ■ Over 150,000 sq. ft. (8)
- ■ 75,000 to 150,000 sq. ft. (10)
- □ Under 75,000 sq. ft. (15)

✕ **WHOLESALE BRANCHES (23)**

NORTHERN STORES:
- ● Junior Department Stores (79)
- ○ Isolated Stores (138)
- ▲ Raw Fur Departments (12)

✳ **FUR AUCTIONS (2)**

Includes Morgan's Stores in Montreal (5) Ottawa (1) and Toronto (1).

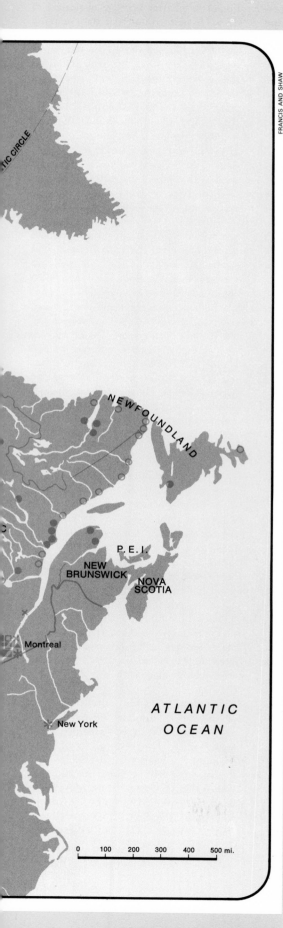

With the sale of 95 per cent of its huge land holdings to the Dominion of Canada in 1870, H.B.C. began the transformation of its factors and traders from profit-sharing officers to salaried executives. The process was completed by 1893, six years after the last council meeting of those officers in Winnipeg (above). Thus a fur-trading post evolved into a diversified sales corporation.

As the map at left suggests, "the Bay" today means to Canadians what "Sears" or "Monkey Ward's" retail department stores do to Americans. You can buy almost anything there, including an exclusive H.B.C. brand of Scotch whisky ("there's a taste of history in every drop"). You can still buy furs, too, although they are as likely to be kidskin or lamb as beaver; and H.B.C. models (above) would have startled an old trapper right out of his sleeping bag.

than twenty thousand pounds a year produced annual profits ranging from four thousand to ten thousand pounds, to be distributed among fewer than a hundred stockholders.

It was a false security. The French, too, recouped. From Montreal, North America's greatest family of adventurers, Pierre Gaultier de Varennes, Sieur de La Vérendrye, his three sons, and a nephew, launched a new drive into the heartland. First they created a staging depot at Grand Portage on the western shore of Lake Superior, so that goods could be stored there during the winter and then rushed ahead as soon as the ice went out of the rivers. Because food was always a major problem for the hurrying boatmen, the Vérendryes built supporting posts at Rainy Lake and Lake of the Woods, where their men raised crops and bought wild rice from the Indians. They improved the arduous portage trails and used missionaries to help bring peace to the warring tribes. Their wilderness diplomacy sometimes backfired. Hoping to woo the Cree away from York Factory, La Vérendrye let one of his boys march with a Cree war party against the Sioux. In vengeance the Sioux later massacred twenty-one Frenchmen, including La Vérendrye's eldest son. The French wanted beaver? Very well, here was some—and the Indians wrapped the decapitated heads of the slain men in beaver pelts for La Vérendrye to find.

In spite of such shocks La Vérendrye kept pushing west. By the middle of the 1740's the family combine had posts south and west of Lake Winnipeg. Unlicensed *coureurs de bois* kept pace with them, and soon the number of choice pelts reaching York Factory dropped by one third.

Attacks at home were added to those in the field. Arthur Dobbs, Surveyor-General of Ireland and the company's most dedicated critic, urged the abrogation of its charter because of neglect of duty. He pointed out that the company was not searching for the Northwest Passage from Hudson Bay to the Pacific. It had allowed the French to establish themselves in its own territories, thus sacrificing trade that would have stimulated employment in English factories. And on and on, until Parliament, squirming under the goad, first offered a reward of twenty thousand pounds to whoever found the passage—Dobbs promptly tried with two ships, but failed—and next, in 1749, ordered a full-scale investigation of the company's activities.

In answer to the hostile inquiries, the company cited the trips its men had made—Kelsey's to the plains, and sporadic ventures along the bay's north coast, during one of which the resident governor James Knight and the crews of two small sloops had died horribly in the ice. In 1743, furthermore, Joseph Isbister of Fort Albany had countered French activity north of Lake Superior by building Henley House at the forks of the Albany River. Henley was a meager place, only about one hundred and forty miles from salt water, but historic nevertheless, for it was the company's first inland post.

The charter survived. Unfortunately, victory in Parliament restored complacency in North America. When Anthony Henday was sent to the foot of the Rockies in 1754, it was in furtherance of the old bankrupt policy: find new Indians and bring them to the bay. He failed. The horse-riding Blackfeet whom he met told him that they did not understand canoes and, furthermore, that they hated fish, which they would have to eat if they left the plains. They would rather stay in their own country, feast on buffalo meat, and buy such goods as they needed from the Cree and Assiniboin, middlemen who traded with the French to the east.

Convinced that the cultural patterns of the Plains Indians could not be changed, Henday urged his employers to change theirs. They declined to take him seriously. He was not a reliable observer, they decided. He said that he had seen Indians on horseback, though everyone knew there were no horses in the western wilderness. Besides, the French were finished. A new war had erupted. In

Three furry partners of the company: the beaver, the seal, and the polar bear (with Eskimo hunter)

24

1759 Quebec fell to Wolfe; and in 1763 the Peace of Paris removed France entirely from North America. At last the field was clear—or so it seemed.

Disabusement came swiftly. Into the vacuum left by the French rushed a new horde of exploiters—Scotsmen, English, and men from the American colonies. At first the chaos of the invasion hid the extent of its threat. The newcomers struggled ferociously with one another for supremacy. They lived hand-to-mouth on shaky credit, debauched the Indians with drink, raided one another's posts, and occasionally killed one another.

The London committee of the Hudson's Bay Company sniffed at the rabble as "Pedlars," but their traders in the field were alarmed. The Pedlars might be at each other's throats, but among them they were getting even more furs than the French had. The time had arrived when the company must exploit its shorter trade routes from the bay and move into the interior ahead of the enemy.

London finally agreed. New outposts were scattered from Henley House southward toward Lake Superior. More vitally, in 1774 Cumberland House was built well up the Saskatchewan by Samuel Hearne, a young explorer who had recently achieved renown for his harrowing overland trip to the mouth of the Coppermine River on the Arctic Ocean. Now let the Pedlars come!

They did, in dismaying force. A league of Montreal merchants strong enough to command ample credit in London linked themselves to the traders, who were called "wintering partners." Ruthlessly this group stamped out internal competition and emerged as the famed North West Company of Canada. Aggressiveness was fostered by giving key field men shares in the firm, a profit incentive that the traders of the Hudson's Bay Company lacked.

Nowhere did the zest produce more spectacular results than in the new company's transportation system. Canoes forty feet long, aided later by tiny sailing ships, carried cargo to the distribution center of Grand Portage on the west side of Lake Superior. (After Grand Portage was found to be in American territory, the center was shifted forty miles northward to Fort William on the Kamanistiquia River.) There the bales of mer-

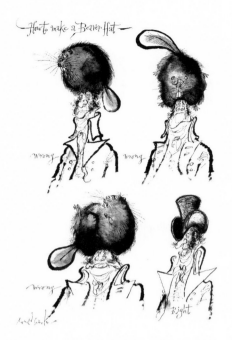

A heady fate awaited most H.B.C. beaver pelts.

chandise were reloaded onto smaller canoes for transport over hundreds of miles of white water to posts as far away as Athabasca and, somewhat later, New Caledonia, beyond the Rockies.*

One essential to the system was the skill and staying power of the singing French-Canadian *voyageurs* from the St. Lawrence. Another was concentrated food for sustaining the paddlers on their heroic journeys. West of Rainy Lake they relied chiefly on pemmican made of dried buffalo meat pounded into a powder and mixed with melted fat. The center for the preparation of pemmican was the prairie land south and southwest of Lake Winnipeg, along the Red River and its tributaries.

By keeping this far-flung network operating smoothly, the Nor'Westers grew into a giant combine that each year exported six or seven times as many furs as the Hudson's Bay Company. And yet the headlong expansion bred its own problems, including a host of young clerks clamoring for a share of the profits, a demand that could be met only by further growth. At that point the fragile

*The Athabasca country lay in what is now northern Alberta Province and stretched west to the Rockies. New Caledonia became British Columbia.

canoes showed their limitations. Additional posts in the Canadian west could not be serviced from Montreal.

A search for a usable river outlet to the Pacific began. After a false cast to the Arctic in 1789, Alexander Mackenzie finally managed, in 1793, to traverse the formidable mountains of today's British Columbia and reach salt water at Bella Coola Sound. Although a tremendous feat of exploration, it solved no problems; the canyons that Mackenzie travelled would never do for boat transport. And so a fight began to force the Hudson's Bay Company to share the river ports of its jealously guarded inland sea.

At the outset of the struggle the English company appeared much weaker than its opponent. Though it had developed shallow-draft overgrown rowboats equipped with sails for quiet water —York boats, they were called—and had imported sturdy Orkneymen from Scotland for manning them, its traders generally reached the Indians half a jump behind the rampaging Nor'Westers. The bulk of the choicest lightweight furs still went to Montreal, leaving the company to barter for the heavier, coarser pelts—skins difficult to market during the dislocations of the Napoleonic wars.

There was one strength, however. The company's stockholders did not have to live on their dividends, as the Nor'Westers did. They had waited out trouble before, and they did so now. Unable to stampede them by public attacks on their charter, Mackenzie next sought, with the financial backing of Thomas Douglas, Earl of Selkirk, to buy control of the company. That effort also failed, mainly because of a clash between Mackenzie and Selkirk over policies to be followed in the event of success.

After the collapse of the venture Selkirk found himself with considerable company stock on hand. Promptly he set about familiarizing himself with the business. One weakness struck him hard— that ancient charter. How could its validity be established against future attack?

He devised an extraordinary plan. He was already committed to setting up colonies in Canada where impoverished Highlanders from Scotland might begin their lives anew. The company charter allowed the formation of colonies on company land. Very well, then. He would obtain a tract from the company, and by planting a colony on it would help his Highlanders while affirming the charter. There would be other benefits. The colonists would grow food for the company's posts and boat crews. They would furnish a pool of manpower on which the company would draw.

The area he selected lay south of Lake Winnipeg. The first colonists, travelling with great hardship through Hudson Bay, reached the site of their intended village near the junction of the Red and Assiniboine rivers (Winnipeg stands there today) in 1812. (See "The Boy Artist of Red River" in the February, 1970, AMERICAN HERITAGE.) It was a choice spot, but it lay in the heart of the Nor'Westers' pemmican country. No matter what Selkirk said about his humanitarianism, to the North West Company the colony looked like a flagrant attempt to disrupt their provisioning routines and thus cripple their transportation system. They reacted explosively.

In 1815 a gang of métis, the half-breed buffalo hunters of the North West Company, burned the colony's huts and trampled its crops. The terrified settlers fled toward York Factory. On the way they met flamboyant Colin Robertson, a one-time Nor'Wester who had deserted to the Hudson's Bay Company. Defiantly Robertson brought the fugitives back to Red River. During the tense winter that followed, he imprisoned Duncan Cameron, the "wintering partner" in charge of the Nor'Westers' nearby Fort Gibraltar. Later the governor of the Selkirk colony, Robert Semple, razed the structure itself.

As soon as spring made travel possible, the Nor'Westers began gathering to free Cameron. Before they reached the settlement, however, the métis struck again— the infamous "Massacre of Seven Oaks." During the carnage Semple and twenty-one settlers died.

Selkirk, who was on his way to Red River with a guard of mercenary soldiers, retaliated by seizing the Nor'Westers' great staging depot, Fort William, on Lake Superior. Simultaneously the traders in the fur country plunged into mutually exhausting campaigns of harassment and disruption.

The British government at Quebec sent investigators into the field. Parliament resounded with charges and coun-

tercharges. In Quebec, as well as in Montreal, the battle seemed a draw, but in the wilderness the Nor'Westers broke.

The North West Company had over-extended in order to build forts in New Caledonia and to buy, during the War of 1812, John Jacob Astor's post of Astoria at the mouth of the Columbia River. It was impossible to digest that expansion while carrying on a wasteful feud. Disgusted by dwindling profits and by the unyielding belligerence of the firm's Montreal agents, winterers John McLoughlin, a towering six feet four inches tall, and Angus Bethune led a revolt in search of peace.

The upshot, after intricate maneuvering, was a union of the two companies. Although the former winterers of the North West Company placed more of their men in responsible positions in the field than did the English company and won a profit-sharing arrangement for all principal workers, the name of the new continent-wide firm was familiar: the Hudson's Bay Company. Management stayed in London; London appointed the resident governor. Aided by the inevitabilities of geography, the little David of the North had swallowed Goliath.

The new resident governor was pudgy George Simpson, a meticulously trained, disagreeably cocky one-time sugar broker's clerk from London. Except for a hard winter in Athabasca during the final year of the conflict, he had had no experience in the fur trade. But he was aboil with energy, and he had a genius for organization.

He reassessed every post from Labrador to New Caledonia, let some stand, moved a few, closed several. He demanded that those in kindly climates grow enough vegetables and livestock to feed themselves. He instituted new transport systems, sending ships around Cape Horn to supply the Columbia district and using York boats out of Hudson Bay to service the posts in the interior. The colorful canoe brigades from Montreal were abandoned, a sore blow to the economy of Lower Canada but an inevitable move for a firm devoted to paring costs.

Expansion continued, more methodically now. Robert Campbell opened the Yukon. Sailing ships, and later a steamboat, plied the north Pacific coast, buy-

ing sea otter from the Indians. A trade in salmon and timber was developed with San Francisco and Hawaii. The Puget Sound Agricultural Company, managed by John McLoughlin, the benevolent chief factor of Fort Vancouver on the Columbia, was formed to provide Russian Alaska with meat, grain, and dairy products.

When American trappers sought to invade the Oregon country, they were easily held back by roving brigades under Peter Skene Ogden and, later, John Work. Settlers were something else. Spearheaded by missionaries to the Indians, they poured into Oregon during the early 1840's, bought supplies on credit from McLoughlin, and then, seeking undivided American jurisdiction over the area (instead of joint sovereignty with Great Britain), raised loud clamors against the company's autocratic ways. Beset by other crises in international affairs, the British government in 1846 yielded to President Polk and let the boundary between the countries be drawn at the forty-ninth parallel, save for the overlapping southern tip of Vancouver Island. There, at Fort Victoria, McLoughlin having resigned to become an American citizen, James Douglas established the company's new western headquarters.

The filling up of Oregon was a harbinger. In 1858 discoveries of gold along the Fraser River brought a stampede of miners into British Columbia. Far to the east lumberjacks invaded the Canadian Shield and augmented their income by trapping in defiance of the company's monopolistic rights. In the Midwest the métis of the Red River regularly left their little farms to smuggle furs to buyers in Minnesota.

The Indians, too, were retreating before the thrusts of civilization, and soon it was clear that a fur empire and population centers could not exist side by side. Suggestions began to be heard that Rupert's Land (the Hudson Bay watershed) be annexed to Canada, a name then applied to the eastern provinces only.

The company reluctantly agreed in principle but asked £1,500,000 in payment. An impasse developed. Canada could not raise the sum, and the French of Quebec, fearing dilution of their political strength, did not want the land anyway. Expansionists tried to break through the money barrier by suggesting that the Crown, which had alienated the land long ago by giving it to the company, was now obligated to buy it back. England resisted. She did not wish to purchase a large block of land and then, if annexation failed to develop, be left to administer a treasury-draining crown colony.

The sentiment for a coast-to-coast confederation of Canada was growing, however, and it was unlikely that a monopolistic landholding of such gargantuan proportions would be allowed to remain undisturbed. Taking advantage of the current, an investment company known as the International Financial Society startled the business world in 1863 by purchasing control of the Hudson's Bay Company. It reorganized the firm under a new set of officers, increased its capitalization, and offered stock to the public with promises of quick profits from the sale of land to settlers. The promoters then pulled out, having reaped a goodly sum from their manipulations.

The company's new board of directors soon realized that the tide of immigration was not yet as strong as they had been led to believe. As its new stockholders grew increasingly indignant over the failure of the land to move, the directors became more and more anxious to sell to either Canada or England—but not at just any price. And so the three-way dickering went on: Who should pay, and how much?

The situation grew intolerable. The American Midwest was filling with settlers, and Canadians feared a northward thrust by their acquisitive neighbors unless defensive measures were taken by someone stronger than the company. At the same time demands were increasing for a cross-country railroad, which, of course, could not be built through privately held land. Abruptly, in 1869, the British government solved matters by imposing terms that the company's board of directors did not like but that they accepted rather than face a long legal battle. Under this settlement, called the Deed of Surrender, the company retained its trading rights but sold nineteen twentieths of Rupert's Land, the so-called Fertile Belt, to Great Britain for £300,000. H.B.C. kept one twentieth—

part of the Fertile Belt in the west—to sell for settlement. Britain then allowed Canada, which had become a confederated dominion in 1867, to annex the entire area.

As its land commissioner to sell off the reserved one twentieth of its former holdings (some seven million acres), the directors chose lean, hard, bushy-browed Donald A. Smith, a one-time fur trader in Labrador and former manager of the company's Montreal district. He had scant success at first. Immigrants preferred the better-advertised fields of the American West. To help turn the tide northward (and to reap profits for himself, an activity that always commanded his exuberant attention), Smith became one of the prime movers of the Canadian Pacific Railroad. Meanwhile he acquired enough stock in the Hudson's Bay Company so that in 1889, when he was sixty-nine, he was able to have himself elected governor in London. He was the first field man ever to attain that exalted rank.

At the turn of the century, when the arable lands of the United States were finally filled, the long-awaited rush into south-central Canada began. Millions of acres of company land sold at such fine prices that in 1906–07 stock dividends approached 50 per cent for the first time since 1688. The success was so great, indeed, that for a time it blinded Smith to another source of income inherent in the headlong growth of the Canadian West —the turning of one-time trading posts into retail stores. The company's sagging forts and the town lots it was offering for sale were almost completely surrounded by aggressive merchants who were making good profits. Finally the board jarred itself awake, and in 1910 it started a series of studies designed to transform primitive systems of bartering into the sophisticated routines of modern retailing.

The company's first two block-sized department stores, both several stories high, were built in 1913 in Vancouver and Calgary. A few months later, in January, 1914, Donald Smith, honored now as Lord Mount Royal and Strathcona, died at the age of ninety-four. In the long span of his governorship his company once again had managed, as so often before, to catch up with its competitors.

The First World War interrupted the building program—but at no loss to the

Hudson's Bay Company, which used its international trading organization to purchase and transport mountains of supplies for France and Russia. When the conflict ended, land sales boomed again. This time the company matched the population growth with a swift expansion of its retail and mail-order facilities. In 1931 supervision of the chain of stores was shifted from London to a subdirectorate with headquarters in Winnipeg.

Surprisingly, the changes did not bring about as dismal a drop in fur-trade

Today the Bay sells refrigerators to Eskimos.

revenues as Smith himself had once predicted. Using light planes for swift communication and tractors and snowmobiles for pulling trains of sleds, the company today has pushed its trading posts to the edges of the Arctic Ocean and has developed a flourishing commerce with the Eskimos. Radisson and Groseilliers would have approved. After all, in the three hundred years since they launched the company, that has been the one unswerving goal—finding and pleasing the customers, whether in wigwams, igloos, or modern apartment houses.

David Lavender is a frequent contributor and the author of several books on the American West, of which the most recent is The Rockies *(Harper & Row, 1968).*

For further reading: Hudson's Bay Company, *by E. E. Rich (3 volumes; Macmillan, 1961);* The Honourable Company, *by Douglas MacKay (Bobbs-Merrill, 1936).*

THE PRESIDENT, THE PEOPLE,

The Constitution of the United States declares in the plainest possible English: "The Congress shall have Power . . . To declare War." Yet in the last twenty years Americans have fought two major wars—in Korea and in Vietnam—without a congressional declaration of war. Apart from the question of who has the right to send the armed forces into serious combat action, Vietnam has been a glaring instance of momentous foreign policy carried out with only the most cursory control by Congress.

Naturally, many Americans opposed to the Vietnam war are crying outrage. Many others, for or against the war or somewhere in between, ask a worried question: What has happened to the traditional constitutional procedure whereby the President leads in international affairs but Congress has a potent check on him when the decision involves life and death for the nation's young men and sweeping consequences for the whole country? Is there no way to bring foreign policy back under greater popular control, by restoring the congressional role or through some other technique?

On the surface, the questions have clear-cut answers, most of which revolve around the contention that particular recent Presidents simply have refused to play by the constitutional rules. Yet in actuality the answers are entangled in complex considerations of just what the Founding Fathers did and did not write into the Constitution, how their decisions have been put into practice over two centuries, and whether the circumstances of warmaking have not changed so much that some of the basic old rules simply do not apply.

The wise and hardheaded men who assembled in 1787 to write a constitution for the United States were members of a generation that had just fought a bitter war against the British executive, King George III. They were sick of battles and their devastation and intensely concerned to circumscribe any decision for war. A gangling freshman congressman from Illinois, denouncing the Mexican-American War a half century later, stated the mood of most of the Founding Fathers as accurately as any historian can. Representative Abraham Lincoln wrote in 1848 that the Constitutional Convention gave the warmaking power to Congress because "kings had always been involving and impoverishing their people in wars, pretending generally, if not always, that the good of the people was the object. This, our Convention under-

stood to be the most oppressive of all kingly oppressions; and they resolved to so frame the Constitution that *no one man* should hold the power of bringing this oppression upon us." (The italics are Lincoln's.)

So the Congress, not the President, was to decide war or peace. But the Founding Fathers lived in an era filled with violence between countries that was not formal war. The new nation would be at a sharp disadvantage if, in the event of depredations against its commerce or maraudings on its land, its armed forces were immobilized until congressmen could gather from thirteen states in their horse-drawn vehicles. The Founding Fathers made one man who was on the scene, the President, Commander in Chief of the Army and Navy. The wording of the first draft of the Constitution gave Congress the exclusive power to "make" war. On the floor of the convention, "make" was changed to "declare," assigning the President the right to use the Army and Navy in order to meet specific emergencies while retaining for the House and Senate the power to decide full-scale war.

The Constitution has often been called a bundle of compromises, and so it was—not least between those who wanted a strong and those who wanted a weak Chief Executive. The Founding Fathers may have made the President the Commander in Chief, but they gave Congress the power of the purse in determining the size and nature of the armed forces. Until late in the convention, the right to make treaties was vested in the Senate alone. But there were obvious advantages in having one man initiate treaties, receive foreign ambassadors, name and instruct American ambassadors. The Chief Executive would do these things, although he was to appoint ambassadors only with the approval of a Senate majority and make treaties with the "Advice and Consent" of two thirds of the Senate.

In foreign affairs, as in all areas, the Founding Fathers were notably spare in laying down specific dictates and in the language that they used to write the provisions. Yet they said enough to make it clear that they envisaged a foreign policy system in which the President would lead, but in collaboration with Congress, especially the Senate, and in which the Chief Executive would be subject to continuing scrutiny and formidable restraints whenever his activities touched that most serious aspect of foreign affairs, general war.

AND THE POWER TO MAKE WAR

On August 22, 1789, President George Washington, sound Constitutionalist that he was, appeared with his Secretary of War in the Senate chamber to "advise" with the senators on a treaty with the southern Indians and to seek their "consent." The reading of the document began. The wasp-tempered Senator William Maclay, from the back country of Pennsylvania, was annoyed because the passing carriages made it difficult for him to hear the words; he and other senators, in the process of forming an agrarian political opposition to President Washington, were ready to be annoyed at anything that came from this administration with its "monarchical" tendencies. The President wanted an immediate vote, but the Maclay group called for time to study the documents connected with the treaty. George Washington, according to Maclay, "started up in a violent fret." Had he not brought along the Secretary of War precisely to answer any questions that might arise? President Washington calmed down, the delay was granted, the treaty was ratified. But Maclay wrote in his diary, "The President wishes to tread on the necks of the Senate. . . . This will not do with Americans." As for George Washington, he is said to have let it be known that "he would be damned if he ever went there again." He did not go there again for advice on a treaty, and neither did any other President.

The clash over this minor document was a preview of the coming years, when the collaboration between the Chief Executive and the Congress, in the case of treaties or other aspects of international affairs, proved prickly and at times violent. Inevitably, Presidents tended to feel that they had superior information and were acting only after mature consideration of the matter; congressmen were interfering out of impulse, ignorance, politics, or a yen to encroach on White House prerogatives. Inevitably, congressmen, considering themselves sound in judgment and closer to the popular will, tended to believe that Chief Executives were trying, as Senator Maclay had declared, to create situations in which "advices and consents [would be] ravished, in a degree, from us."

Before many decades it also became clear that while Congress might have the war power, a determined Chief Executive could put the House and the Senate in a position where they had little alternative except to vote war. The Democratic President elected in 1844, the unsmiling, tenacious James K. Polk, believed it was manifest destiny for America to expand. Texas had been formally annexed, but Mexico still considered it a rebellious province, and border disputes continued; California lay a luscious plum ready for the plucking from Mexico. President Polk kept trying to maneuver Mexico into acceptance of his ambitions, while he built a fervid public opinion behind expansionism. Finally the President ordered General Zachary Taylor into territory claimed by Mexico, and Mexican troops attacked American cavalry, killing or wounding sixteen.

On Sunday, May 10, 1846, President Polk went to church but, as he put it, "regretted" that he had to spend the rest of the Sabbath on a quite different matter —working out a war bill and a strategy for Congress. The measure provided an appropriation of ten million dollars and the calling up of fifty thousand volunteers. The disciplined Democratic majority in the House of Representatives limited debate to two hours, and only in the last minutes did the Polk leaders present a preamble to the bill that was a declaration of war. The House and the Senate included a strong anti-war faction. But now all members were in the position where they either voted for the whole measure or—with a good deal of public opinion near hysteria—voted against money and troops for General Taylor's forces. The House approved, 174–14; the Senate, 40–2.

Those dogged fourteen Noes in the House included ex-President John Quincy Adams; and Representative Abraham Lincoln, just arrived in Washington, would soon begin his sharpshooting against the war. Major intellectuals joined in the assault. Henry Thoreau spent a night in the Concord lockup for refusing to pay his poll tax in protest, and when his aunt paid the money, much to his annoyance, he went back to Walden Pond and wrote his famous essay "Civil Disobedience." The agitation went on, but within five months American troops were swinging along the plaza of Mexico City, gazing in awe and in triumph at the great baroque cathedral and the pink walls of the Halls of Montezuma, asserting by their mud-spattered presence that President Polk was about to achieve in abundance the territorial acquisitions he sought.

Half a century later the obverse of the coin was showing. Of all wars the United States has fought, none has come to be considered more pointless and reprehensible than the Spanish-American War, and that venture was the doing of Congress, driven on by public opinion. During the 1890's a rebellion in the Spanish colony of Cuba, brutally combatted by the Madrid government, caught up a mounting jingo sentiment in the United States. Before long the principal opponents of armed intervention were the American businessmen owning property in Cuba, who wanted things settled without dislocating their economic arrangements, and the two Presidents of the era, Grover Cleveland and William McKinley.

When Congress roared through a resolution recognizing the "belligerency" of the Cuban rebels, President Cleveland denounced the move as an intrusion on the powers of the Chief Executive and privately remarked that if Congress declared war, he as Commander in Chief would refuse to mobilize the Army. President McKinley tried, too; he undertook negotiations with Madrid to bring better treatment of the rebels. But the popular uproar, stoked by tabloid papers, kept increasing. William McKinley's face grew haggard from the pills he was taking trying to get to sleep; once he sat on a big crimson brocade lounge in the White House and burst into tears as he spoke of the way Congress was forcing the country into war. Finally, the President capitulated. He planned to run for re-election; besides, he was scarcely deaf to voices like that of the senator who thundered to Assistant Secretary of State William R. Day, "Day, by ——, don't your President know where the war-declaring power is lodged? Tell him by ——, that if he doesn't do something, Congress will exercise the power." President McKinley sat working on a war message as the Spanish government conceded major American demands—a concession made before the message actually reached the House and the Senate—and he added poignantly that he hoped Congress would give the Spanish terms "just and careful attention."

A war of territorial seizure maneuvered through by a determined President, an ugly war forced by public opinion and Congress, six wars or significant uses of the armed forces in a little more than a hundred years, more and more instances of acrid White House-Congress clashes in foreign affairs—during the late eighteenth and nineteenth centuries the constitutional system was hardly functioning with glowing results in international matters. Yet the wars or quasi-wars did not pile up long casualty lists; they did not slash through everyday living. The most disruptive conflict, the Civil War, was removed by its very nature from the usual questions of constitutional responsibility. Whatever the underlying reality, even the Mexican-American War was fought under an authorization overwhelmingly granted by Congress. If the wars created savage debates, they spread little bitter feeling that questions of life and death were too far removed from grass-roots control.

President Theodore Roosevelt has often been called "the first modern President," and he was that in many ways. In international affairs the world was taking on its twentieth-century form of great powers jockeying for global position, vast economic stakes overseas, and armed forces designed to strike swiftly. These trends inevitably centered more foreign policy power in the hands of the American President, who was far more able than the cumbersome Congress to operate in this kind of arena. The rambunctious Teddy Roosevelt, no man to turn away from power, responded by driving deep into the American system the doctrine that the Chief Executive is—to use his phrase—"the steward" of the nation, endowed under the Constitution with vast "inherent powers" to act in behalf of what he considers the good of the country.

Action accompanied doctrine. Did T.R. deem it to be in the national interest for the United States to have a canal across Central America so that the Navy could be moved quickly from one ocean to another, and was the Colombian government proving balky? In 1903 T.R. saw to it that Panamanian rebels set up an independent state covering the desired canal zone, and the new nation, to no one's surprise, gave him what he wanted. ("I took the Canal Zone," said President Theodore Roosevelt, "and let Congress debate.") Did T.R. arrive at the conclusion during the Russo-Japanese War of 1904-05 that the security of the United States was best served by a Japanese victory? In entire secrecy he informed Tokyo that, if needed, America would act as an ally, which could have proved a commitment for war. Did the triumphant Japanese then seem a bit too cocky? In 1907 T.R. ordered the entire American fleet on a razzle-dazzle trip around the world, loosing all kinds of diplomatic reverberations. Congressional opponents stirred, particularly those from eastern regions fearing the lack of naval protection, and they talked of denying the appropriation for the fleet movement. Very well, T.R. replied. He had enough money to send the ships to the Pacific Coast, and they could stay there.

It was all very much Teddy Roosevelt, and more than a little rococo. Yet this first modern President was also anticipating in a serious way the modern presidential trend. Stirred on by changed conditions, he was moving through that broad arch erected by the Founding Fathers—between, on the one side, the clear power of the Chief Executive to lead in foreign affairs and to command the armed forces and, on the other side, the powers of Congress to do certain specific things.

As the twentieth century progressed and the enmeshments of the world grew tighter and more troublesome, Presidents probed still more vigorously the limits of the arch. This development was not only implicit in the circumstances; it was furthered by the difference between the vantage of the Chief Executive and the Congress. The President felt full blast the forces of modernity, which came crashing daily into his office. As the leader of the whole nation, he was heavily influenced by considerations of collective security, the moral position of the United States before international opinion, and the problems that tied in with the stability of the country's economy. Of course members of Congress knew these same concerns, but they were also subject to local, more inward-looking pressures. The House and the Senate continued to include strong blocs which represented the decades-old view that the business of America is America and which resented the persistent intrusion of the world. The abrasion between the two ends of Pennsylvania Avenue in matters of foreign policy sharpened. More and more, Presidents viewed Congress as the adversary and thought in terms of skirting around it or, if necessary, ignoring it.

This occurred at critical points on the road toward American participation in both World Wars I and II. During the European phase of World War I, Germany climaxed three years of friction with the United States by announcing unrestricted submarine warfare. President Wilson had long been troubled by considerations of the moral position of the United States with respect to the conflict, and the feeling of his responsibility to assert American rights on the high seas; now he could not overlook the fact that hundreds of ships, fearful of submarines, were clinging to port and great supplies of wheat and cotton were piling up, threatening to dislocate the nation's economic life. In February, 1917, President Wilson asked Congress for authority to arm merchantmen, an act that could scarcely fail to lead to war. The debate was stormy, and in the upper house eleven senators filibustered the measure to death. Thereupon the President announced that "a little group of willful men had rendered the great government of the United States helpless and contemptible" and ordered the merchantmen armed anyhow. War was declared in April.

After the eruption of the second European war in 1939 President Franklin Roosevelt was convinced that for the good of the United States it belonged at the side of the antifascist powers. Yet he faced tremendous anti-intervention sentiment, so amply reflected in Congress that as late as the summer of 1941, a year after the fall of France, the House extended the draft law by exactly one vote. Under the circumstances, F.D.R. undertook an extraordinary series of executive actions, which sought to hem in Japan economically and to help the nations fighting Nazi Germany. Weeks before Pearl Harbor these moves included an order that in effect meant convoying—despite a congressional ban on convoying—and an order to the Army Air Forces and the Navy to shoot first at German and Italian vessels found in the western Atlantic, which amounted to *de facto* warfare.

By the time America was fighting in World War II, it was manifest that President Roosevelt had made war and was continuing to conduct foreign policy with only a defensive concern for congressional opinion. Plenty of angry comment was made about this, yet still the warmaking power did not become a major national issue. In the case of both World Wars I and II, a semblance of congressional authority was preserved by the ultimate declarations of war voted by the House and Senate. Of more significance, the two wars were generally accepted by the public; they were led by widely popular Chief Executives; and if they brought serious problems to the society, they did not seem to tear it apart.

In June, 1950, President Harry Truman was visiting his Missouri home when he learned of the invasion of South Korea by North Korea. Flying back to Washington, he mulled over the news. This was plain aggression, the President told himself; aggression unchecked during the 1930's had led to World War II; he was not going to be party to another such tragedy. The next morning the reports were grim: South Korea appeared about to collapse. That night Harry Truman ordered American armed forces into the Korean fighting. Then the United Nations Security Council, on motion of the United States representative, "recommended" assistance to South Korea, and the President summoned congressional leaders, as he put it, "so that I might inform them on the events and decisions of the past few days." The Korean War was under way, grinding on for more than three years, costing the nation 33,629 battle deaths and 103,284 wounded. At no time did President Truman ask congressional authority for the war.

Behind this White House attitude were all the reasons that had been accumulating for decades. But other and profoundly important elements had also entered into the relationship between the Chief Executive and Congress in the conduct of foreign affairs. The simple fact was that the traditional concept of a President leading in foreign policy and then, if necessary, going to Congress for a declaration of war had become obsolete. Historically, war meant that a nation, using whatever weapons seemed feasible, attempted to conquer another country or to beat it into submission. In an era of Cold War, and after the development of nuclear weapons, armed conflicts were taking a different form. Small Communist nations, unofficially backed by large ones, were probing remote areas. The United States was replying not by war in the conventional sense but by what was being called "limited war"—limited in the use of weapons because nuclear power was ruled out and limited in objective, which was not to crush the enemy but to stop him from spreading Communism and to discourage similar efforts in the future.

All the while, the relationship of war to the home front was altering. By the 1950's the United States was so complex a society and Washington so overweening a force that a declaration of war had immense impact. This was partly psychological, but it also involved fundamental workaday facts. Over the decades, by laws and even more by precedents, a declaration of war had come to confer on the President sweeping powers over the entire national life, particularly in the sensitive area of economic affairs. Fighting a limited war, President Truman wanted to limit its home effects, and the opposition to them which could be so easily aroused.

So President Harry Truman went on fighting the Korean War on the authority of President Harry Truman. At times he spoke of the "authorization" or "summons" resulting from the action of the U.N. Security Council; the references were not taken too seriously. The war took calamitous turns. It exacerbated American social problems that were already serious. The very idea of "limited war"—"fighting a war with one hand tied behind you," as people said—ground on the nerves of a nation accustomed to striding in for the knockout. Public opinion, which at first strongly favored the Korean intervention, swung against it and to an extent that had not occurred during any previous conflict; by 1951 the Gallup poll reported a majority believing that the whole intervention was a mistake and favoring prompt withdrawal. Opposition leaders in Congress now were storming against "Truman's War," that "unconstitutional" war; and this time the attacks were building a feeling that something was definitely wrong with the warmaking procedures of the United States.

After the Korean War, and as part of the mounting American concern over Communist expansionism, the United States stepped up negotiations with other nations for regional defense pacts. These agreements were impeccably constitutional; they were treaties, negotiated by the executive branch, then debated in the Senate and approved by a two-thirds vote. Yet they contained clauses that could be construed to give Presidents further leverage in foreign affairs. A typical pact was SEATO, negotiated in 1954 by the Eisenhower Secretary of State, John Foster Dulles. It bound the United States, in the event of "armed aggression" by a Communist nation in Southeast Asia, to "act to meet the common danger in accordance with its constitutional processes" and, in the case of other types of threats in the area, to "consult" on the measures to be adopted—whatever a President might take all that to mean, in whatever specific circumstances he found himself.

Simultaneously, an old procedure—a joint House-Senate congressional resolution concerning international affairs—was gathering fresh meaning. After the lambasting President Truman took during the Korean War, Presidents who contemplated moves that might result in war or quasi-war sought some form of mandate from the House and the Senate. They also wanted to gather bipartisan support behind their action or projected action and behind their general policy, and—of great importance in their minds—they sought to present a united front to warn off Communist or Communist-allied nations from adventurous plans.

The joint resolutions came in rapid succession: in 1955, when President Eisenhower thought he might use armed forces to protect Formosa from Red China; in 1957, when he was considering intervening in the Middle East to prevent strategic areas from falling under Soviet control; and in 1962, when President Kennedy was maneuvering to isolate Castro's Cuba. The joint resolutions varied in a number of ways. But they were alike in their general pattern of giving congressional approval to a specific action or contemplated action of the Chief Executive and to his broadly stated policy for a particular troubled area of the world.

During the presidential campaign of 1964, the celebrated shots were fired in the Gulf of Tonkin by North Vietnamese gunboats against an American destroyer. A heated debate has broken out concerning just how honest President Lyndon Johnson was in reporting the total episode to the public and concerning the larger circumstances surrounding it. The relevant facts here are that the President believed that he should, by retaliating, discourage the North Vietnamese from any such further attacks; that as a politician running for office, he wanted to underline that he was as anti-Communist as his opponent, Barry Goldwater; that the South Vietnamese situation was disintegrating and he did not know what he might want to do about it in the coming months; that he was acutely aware of what had happened to his friend Harry Truman; and that he did not overlook the potentialities of the new type of regional pacts and joint resolutions.

President Johnson ordered a harsh retaliatory bombing of North Vietnamese patrol-boat bases. Then he summoned congressional leaders and told them he thought a joint resolution, like the Formosa and Middle East and Cuban resolutions, should be put through Congress swiftly. The document reached the House and Senate the next morning. It approved the bombing; spoke of America's "obligations" under SEATO to defend South Vietnam; declared that the United States was "prepared, as the President determines, to take all necessary steps, including the use of armed force," to assist any SEATO nation "in defense of its freedom";

and provided that the resolution remain in force until the Chief Executive declared it no longer necessary or the Congress repealed it by majority votes.

The House devoted most of its time to speeches approving the retaliatory bombing of the previous evening, and Representative Henry S. Reuss, from Milwaukee, said all that could be said on that subject. He was reminded, Reuss observed, of the story about the bartender who called the saloon owner on the intercom and asked, "Is Casey good for a drink?"

"Has he had it?"

"He has."

"He is."

The Senate spent more time on the general authorization granted by the resolution. Members rose to ask, Didn't the language mean that the Congress was empowering the President to take any steps he deemed wise, including waging war, in Southeast Asia? Senator J. William Fulbright, the floor leader for the resolution, and a number of other senators replied that President Johnson had stated that it was his policy not to use combat forces in Southeast Asia; the resolution simply backed this policy; it had to be broad and to be approved quickly to show the North Vietnamese how much the American people, without regard to party, were against armed Communist expansion in Southeast Asia. How many congressmen wanted to vote No on such a proposition, especially three months before an election? The debate on the Tonkin Resolution in the House took just forty minutes, and the tally was 416–0. The Senate, after only eight hours of discussion, approved 88–2.

As President Johnson went on escalating the Vietnam war, he brandished freely the foreign policy powers of the White House, including making executive agreements—some secret—that went well beyond the Truman moves and entangled the United States and Asian countries in ways the full purport of which is still not known. More than the Korean War, Vietnam distorted American society at a time when it was still less able to stand further dislocation. And as a large part of public opinion and of Congress turned against the involvement, the cries once again went up, against "Johnson's war," that "unconstitutional horror." But this time there was a difference.

Lyndon Johnson used to carry the difference around with him on a piece of paper crumpled in his pocket. When the subject of his authority for the war came up, he would pull out the slip containing the Tonkin Resolution and read from it. The two Eisenhower joint resolutions and the Kennedy one had concerned crises that went away, or at least seemed to; the problem treated in the Tonkin Resolution turned into a major war, and L.B.J. exploited the document fully, privately and publicly. On one private occasion, he took it out and read emphatically the resolution's reference to American "obligations" under SEATO. With still more stress, hand clapping on knee, he repeated the phrases that the United States was "prepared, *as the President determines*, to take *all* necessary steps." Lyndon Johnson demanded to know, Did Congress limit its authorization in *any* way? Embittered by the opposition to the war and the personal attacks on him, he continued in a deliberately provocative allusion to nuclear bombs, which he had no intention of using: Did Congress limit at all even *what kind* of weapons he could use? The President put the paper away. Besides, he added, if they have changed their minds, why don't they just vote, as the resolution says, to repeal it?

Lyndon Johnson knew perfectly well that few congressmen would dare face their constituents if, by such a vote for repeal, they undercut a President and a Commander in Chief in the middle of a grave war which he had entered with the insistence that it was vital to American security and world peace. The new regional pacts and even more the joint resolutions—inaugurated with the best of intentions to meet contemporary circumstances—had given the Chief Executive still more war power, and done it in a manner that came close to caricaturing the intent of the Founding Fathers. For they were nothing less than a means by which Congress, with all the whereases of constitutional procedure, duly voted itself into impotence.

In 1967 President Johnson's Under Secretary of State, Nicholas deB. Katzenbach, appeared before the Senate Foreign Relations Committee. His remarks, reflecting the L.B.J. mood, came close to saying that the Chief Executive has the right to do anything he considers best in international matters without regard to Congress. Midway in the testimony a committee member, Senator Eugene J. McCarthy, got up and walked out muttering, "There is only one thing to do—take it to the country." This reaction was a factor in projecting McCarthy into his anti-war presidential candidacy. It was a reaction that was being felt throughout the country—combining discontent with the war and what it was doing to the nation with the charge that President Johnson was manipulating and bulldozing the American people through a war they did not want to fight.

Inevitably, a flood of proposals have come, some for amendments to the Constitution, others for congressional action. Almost all seek to return to Congress—and thus, presumably, closer to "the people"—greater participation in foreign affairs, with the usual assumption that the Congress would be less likely to venture into unwise wars than the President. The most serious of these moves has been a resolution proposed by Senator Fulbright and adopted by the Senate in 1969, which went at one major aspect of the problem through the concept of a "national commitment." It was "the sense of the Senate," the resolution declared, that the United States can make a commitment to a foreign nation only through a specific document agreed upon by both the legislative and executive branches.

But serious doubts are provoked by any of these proposals. The nub of the situation is the power of the Chief Executive as Commander in Chief and those general or "inherent powers" that have come to cluster about the office of the Presidency. Is there really a way to restrict the powers of the Commander in Chief without possibly doing more harm than good in an era when one man's swiftly pressing the button may be necessary for some degree of national survival, or his prompt decision to use non-nuclear armed forces could be essential to achieving a purpose generally agreed upon by the country? Do the words exist that could inhibit "inherent powers" without simultaneously harassing the President, or blocking him, in taking actions that are widely considered necessary? Is this not particularly true in a period when his office is the one instrumentality that can make decisive moves in behalf of the national interest, whether that interest be expressed in domestic or foreign affairs—in orders to armed forces to strike abroad or to enforce federal laws at home, to affect importantly the deployment of economic and social resources inside the country or eight thousand miles away, or to assert at home or abroad the nation's bedrock values? Yet if the proposals do not cut back on any of these essentials, how effectively do they close off the routes by which Presidents have moved independently to war?

The Fulbright resolution concerning "national commitments," for example, might discourage certain kinds of the global wheeler-dealing of a Theodore Roosevelt or a Lyndon Johnson. But the resolution is merely an expression of senatorial opinion; it puts no effective check on a Chief Executive acting as Commander in Chief or wielding "inherent powers." Neither T.R. nor L.B.J. would have considered the basic moves of their foreign policies subject to the resolution, and almost certainly it would not have prevented American entrance into, say, the Vietnam war.

Apart from the difficulty of controlling the President by new language, there is a still more troublesome question—whether, in fact, the Congress and "the people" are less likely than a Chief Executive to get the country into an unwise war. There is not only the glaring instance of the Spanish-American war; other examples, most notably the War of 1812, give pause. Then a rampant faction in Congress—a group with dreams of conquering Canada, who brought the phrase "war hawks" into the American language—helped mightily in pushing the United States into a conflict that was a credit neither to the good sense nor the conscience of the nation. Similarly, in the early, frightened Cold War days, President Truman was worried, and justly so, about a considerable congressional bloc that was restless to take on Russia.

Yet whatever must be said about the dangers or difficulties of restricting the presidential power to make war, the fact remains that something is decidedly wrong with the process as it has emerged full-blown in the 1960's. It *is* a travesty of democracy to have so vital a decision so completely in the hands of one man. As Benjamin Franklin observed during the Constitutional Convention, the nation can never be sure "what sort" of human being will end up in the White House; some might be overly ambitious or "fond of war." The country can also never be certain—no matter how able and peace-minded the Chief Executive—that he will not be led into an unfortunate decision by his dogmas or his limitations. Lyndon Johnson, to use a striking instance, was a Chief Executive of high abilities in a number of respects; he had a strong personal urge to be a peace President and well-seasoned political reasons for avoiding the travail of war. Yet he escalated the Vietnam intervention relentlessly, lashed ahead by old-style certitudes and an inadequate understanding of the forces at work in Asia.

Ideally, what is needed is the creation in modern terms of a system something like the one envisaged by the Founding Fathers, in which the President would have his powers as Commander in Chief and would lead in foreign policy while being guided and checked to some degree by Congress. Toward that end, no good purpose is served by continuing the practice of congressional joint resolutions in international affairs. Either the resolution must say so little that it does not significantly present a bipartisan front to the enemy, or it must be so sweeping that it hands the Chief Executive a blank check.

Beyond this negative suggestion there are all those difficulties in conceiving of a single congressional move that would better the situation. Probably improvement will have to come not by the beguiling expedient of one action but by slower and more complex changes within the existing relationship. For this purpose it is essential to note that in every instance when the United States has gone through all the prescribed constitutional forms, with the President recommending war and the Congress "declaring" it, the House and the Senate have never really "declared war." Five consecutive times, from the War of 1812 through World War II, what Congress actually did was to recognize an existing state of war, allegedly caused by other nations. This was not simply the result of the natural desire to make the enemy appear the cause of the fighting. More importantly, it reflected the facts that by the time Congress considered a declaration of war, a long train of actions had made combat involvement inevitable or next to inevitable and that, in most instances, the actions had been taken by the White House.

The problem of increasing the participation of Congress in foreign policy therefore involves less the matter of a declaration of war than a continuing role for the legislative branch in the decisions that lead to large-scale military intervention. Thinking along these lines, it is useless to assume that the built-in tension between the White House and the Hill can be removed. Yet changes could be made that would increase the degree of genuine collaboration.

All modern Presidents have called in congressmen to "consult" concerning major foreign policy moves. The vital point is the nature of the "consulting." Is it a session in which the Chief Executive really listens to his guests, or is it one in which he is simply informing them of what he proposes to do or has done or, asking their advice, receives it merely with a politeness calculated to grease relations with the Hill? The presidential attitude takes shape from many things, but in no minor degree from the type of men with whom he is talking. And outstanding congressmen can not only influence Presidents; they can rouse opinion in their own chambers and in the nation as a whole, which is certain to have its effects in the White House.

In his *Memoirs* President Truman touched upon the kind of congressional leaders with whom he was dealing during the Korean War. At times bitingly, he indicated how little he thought of the ability of a number of them to rise above narrow-gauged partisanship, of their knowledgeability in world affairs, even of their willingness to observe discretion when the Chief Executive revealed to them information that was necessary for understanding but seriously affected national security.

Truman, a former senator, knew his Congress only too well. For years students of American government have been pointing to the deplorable effects of the seniority system in Congress, and nowhere has it operated more lamentably than in placing men on that critical body for international matters, the Senate Committee on Foreign Relations. In the early twentieth century, when the White House was enormously aggrandizing its power over foreign policy, a number of the senators who were the chairmen or the ranking minority figures on the committee were close to the clownish in their inappropriateness. Since the advent of nuclear weapons, which brought the gravest of issues before the committee, the chairman and first minority senator have at times been able, informed, and dedicated. Yet to run down the list of the number-one and number-two figures since 1945, not to speak of the total makeup of the body, is to come upon some men whose lack of qualifications is staggering.

The problem is not simply one of bringing to the Foreign Relations Committee senators who will command, and justly command, the ear of the President and the country. There is the further consideration of whether they will insist upon equipping themselves with the kind of staff that permits them to operate with knowledge and force. One of the basic reasons for the overweening supremacy of the White House in international affairs has been its machinery for accumulating facts and its capacity to withhold or distort information and to project its interpretations of events. There is no reason why a Congress that took seriously its role, and was backed by the public in its assertiveness, could not establish information machinery that would enable it to fight the battle of Pennsylvania Avenue on more equal terms.

The potential of such congressional action has been strikingly demonstrated in recent years. During the Vietnam debate in the L.B.J. days, the Senate Foreign Relations Committee, headed by the sharp-minded J. William Fulbright and more or less adequately staffed, began to operate like a countervailing power in international matters. Lyndon Johnson may have come to detest William Fulbright, but he read carefully every word the senator said. The committee launched hearings that were a prime factor in building congressional and public opinion against the war and in ultimately changing Johnson policies. Fulbright has apologized for the "perfunctory" attention his committee gave to the Tonkin Resolution in the early days, and the remark is of more than personal significance. It is an open question whether the United States would have ended up fighting in Vietnam if the Senate Foreign Relations Committee had been vigilant, continuously informed, and articulate during the years from 1954 when the essential shape of affairs in Southeast Asia was developing.

The slow and intricate process of building a realistic base for congressional participation in international affairs—will the American people press for it? A natural aftermath of war is the urge to forget about its horrors, including the way that the country got into them. Yet Vietnam has been a shock to millions and to groups containing many influential figures, and certainly the foreseeable trend of events will keep ever present the possibility of large-scale United States combat involvement. Perhaps the present high feelings about Vietnam will carry over sufficiently to create a congressional stance that will give the American people some degree of responsible surveillance over the disposition abroad of their lives, their fortunes, and their sacred honor.

Eric Goldman is Rollins Professor of History at Princeton. From 1963 to 1966 he served in the White House as Special Consultant to the President.

Hard Times

Remembered

By STUDS TERKEL

Mr. Terkel, who has a daily radio show on WFMT *in Chicago, is the author of* Division Street: America. *Published in* 1967, *this study of the lives and feelings of a cross section of Chicagoans quickly became a best seller. In his new book,* Hard Times: An Oral History of the Great Depression, *Mr. Terkel has explored a wider field. He has recorded the memories of hundreds of Americans who lived through the grim decade of the 1930's. Some of their children also express vicarious feelings about those years—years that, in one sense or another, scarred their parents' lives, and created attitudes that the children have come to admire or, just as often, to resent. In* Hard Times, *which will be published later this month by Pantheon Books, Mr. Terkel adds little commentary to the emotions and experiences that his sensitive interviewing elicited. He simply lets his subjects—sometimes famous men, more often ordinary citizens—speak. There are no statistics here. "The precise date is of small consequence," the author writes in his introduction. "In their rememberings are their truths."* AMERICAN HERITAGE *presents a selection of these American voices— remembering.*

Peggy Terry, a child in Oklahoma when the Depression started, now lives in a poor district of Chicago.

I first noticed the difference when we'd come home from school in the evening. My mother'd send us to the soup line. And we were never allowed to cuss. If you happened to be one of the first ones in line, you didn't get anything but water that was on top. So we'd ask the guy that was ladling out the soup into the buckets—everybody had to bring their own bucket to get the soup—he'd dip the greasy, watery stuff off the top. So we'd ask him to please dip down to get some meat and potatoes from the bottom of the kettle. But he wouldn't do it. So we learned to cuss. We'd say: "Dip down, goddammit." . . .

Even after the soup line, there wasn't anything. The W.P.A. came and I married. My husband worked on the W.P.A. We were just kids. I was fifteen and he was sixteen. . . . My husband and me just started travelling around, for about three years. It was a very nice time, because when you're poor and you stay in one spot, trouble just seems to catch up with you. But when you're moving from town to town, you don't stay there long enough for trouble to catch up with you. It's really a good life, if you're poor and you can manage to move around.

I was pregnant when we first started hitchhiking, and people were really very nice to us. Sometimes they would feed us. I remember one time we

In the thirties the Farm Security Administration assigned photographers to make a documentary record of America during the Depression; the great collection, from which all our illustrations are taken, is now in the Library of Congress. These haunting faces are details from some of the most brilliant pictures by Dorothea Lange, Ben Shahn, Arthur Rothstein, and Russell Lee. Individual credits appear on page 44.

AMERICAN HERITAGE BOOK SELECTION

slept in a haystack and the lady of the house came out and found us and she said, "This is really very bad for you because you're going to have a baby. You need a lot of milk." So she took us up to the house.

She had a lot of rugs hanging on the clothesline because she was doing her housecleaning. We told her we'd beat the rugs for giving us the food. She said, no, she didn't expect that. She just wanted to feed us. We said, no, we couldn't take it unless we worked for it. And she let us beat her rugs. I think she had a million rugs, and we cleaned them. Then we went in, and she had a beautiful table, full of all kinds of food and milk. When we left, she filled a gallon bucket full of milk, and we took it with us.

Ward James, seventy-three, is now a teacher in a private boys' school.

. . . I finally went on relief. It's an experience I don't want anybody to go through. It comes as close to crucifixion as . . . You sit in an auditorium and are given a number. The interview was utterly ridiculous and mortifying. In the middle of mine, a more dramatic guy than I dived from the second-floor stairway, head first, to demonstrate he was gonna get on relief even if he had to go to the hospital to do it. There were questions like: Who are your friends? Where have you been living? Where's your family?—I had sent my wife and child to her folks in Ohio, where they could live more simply. Why should anybody give you money? Why should anybody give you a place to sleep? What sort of friends?—This went on for half an hour. I got angry and said, "Do you happen to know what a friend is?" He changed his attitude very shortly. I did get certified some time later. I think they paid nine dollars a month.

I came away feeling I didn't have any business living any more. I was imposing on somebody, a great society or something like that. . . .

Eileen Barth was a county social worker during the Depression.

. . . I'll never forget one of the first families I visited. The father was a railroad man who had lost his job. I was told by my supervisor that I really had to *see* the poverty. If the family needed clothing, I was to investigate how much clothing they had at hand. So I looked into this man's closet (*pauses, it becomes difficult*)—he was a tall, gray-haired man, though not terribly old. He let me look in the closet—he was so insulted (*she weeps angrily*). He said, "Why are you doing this?" I remember his feeling of humiliation . . . this terrible humiliation. (*She can't continue. After a pause, she resumes.*) He said, "I really haven't anything to hide, but if you really must look into it . . ." I could see he was very proud. He was so deeply

humiliated. And I was, too. . . .

Diana Morgan was the daughter of a socially prominent businessman in a small North Carolina town.

The banks failed about the time I was getting ready to go to college. My family thought of my going to Wellesley, Vassar, Smith . . . but we had so little money, we thought of a school in North Carolina. It wasn't so expensive.

It was in my junior year and I came home for Christmas . . . I found the telephone disconnected. And this was when I realized that the world was falling apart. Imagine us without a telephone! When I finished school, I couldn't avoid facing the fact that we didn't have a cook any more, we didn't have a cleaning woman any more. I'd see dust under the beds, which is something I'd never seen before. I knew the curtains weren't as clean as they used to be. Things were beginning to look a little shabby. . . .

Louis Banks, a Negro, is now in a veterans' hospital.

Were there black and white hoboes together?

Yes, it didn't make any difference who you were, 'cause everybody was poor. All friendly, sleep in a jungle. We used to take a big pot and cook food—cabbage, meat, and beans all together. We all set together, we made a tent. Twenty-five or thirty would be out on the side of the rail, white and colored. They didn't have no mothers or sisters, they didn't have no home, they were dirty, they had overalls on, they didn't have no food, they didn't have anything. . . .

Sometimes we sent one hobo to walk, to see if there were any jobs open. He'd come back and say: Detroit, no jobs. He'd say: they're hirin' in New York City. So we went to New York City. Sometimes ten or fifteen of us would be on the train. . . .

Tom Yoder is a recent Notre Dame graduate, whose mother lives in a middle-class house in Evanston, Illinois.

How did you come to your knowledge of the Depression?

(*Smiles slightly, indicating his mother*) I suppose I learned most of it from my parents. My mother has a fantastic story, in my opinion. It seems just absolutely—it's almost in a black-humorous sense—funny to me. To realize that a hundred miles from Chicago, about forty years ago, my mother's brothers, whom I know well now, were out with little rifles, hunting for food to live on. And if they didn't find it, there were truly some empty stomachs. I mean, this is just too much. I don't think my generation can really comprehend what all this means. I've never gone to bed hungry—I wish I had. I haven't and I probably never will.

Whenever I've griped about my home life, Mother's always said, "I hope you always have it so good."

Mary Owsley set out with her husband for Oklahoma in 1929 after he lost his job as a dynamite man in a Kentucky mine.

We lived in a company house. We had to buy every bucket of water we used, 'cause the company undermined things so bad, they ruined all the water wells. I bought my food from the company store, and we bought our furniture from the company store, and we paid three prices on it. I've seen my husband have to borry from his next paycheck what they call scrip, to buy just medicine and things like that. And we didn't live extravagant either. We paid over two-hundred-and-sixty-some-odd dollars for furniture from the coal company. We paid it all back but twenty dollars. And when he went and got another job, he brought a truck down there for the furniture. And they took the whole thing away from us. They wouldn't let us pay the twenty dollars. . . .

Peggy Terry, again, recalls her childhood.

. . . And when my father finally got his bonus, he bought a second-hand car for us to come back to Kentucky in. My dad said to us kids: "All of you get in the car. I want to take you and show you something." On the way over there, he'd talk about how life had been tough for us, and he said: "If you think it's been rough for us, I want you to see people that really had to rough." This was in Oklahoma City, and he took us to one of the Hoovervilles, and that was the most incredible thing.

Here were all these people living in old, rusted-out car bodies. I mean that was their home. There were people living in shacks made of orange crates. One family with a whole lot of kids were living in a piano box. This wasn't just a little section; this was maybe ten miles wide and ten miles long. People living in whatever they could junk together. . . .

Dynamite Garland, forty-five, is now a waitress in Chicago. She formerly danced in burlesque.

Every Sunday we used to go house hunting. That was a recreation during the Depression. You'd get in the Model A with the family and go look at the houses. They were all for sale or rent. You'd go look and see where you could put this and where you could put that, and this is gonna be my room. I knew where I was gonna have my horse in the barn. My mother'd go down in the basement, saying, "Oh, this is well constructed. This is where we're gonna put the potato bin, this is where we're gonna put the onions." We knew just where everyone was gonna be (laughs). . . .

Beside the sad jumble of her household possessions, an evicted share-cropper stands patiently on guard. The photograph was taken in New Madrid County, Missouri, by Arthur Rothstein in 1939.

Tad, twenty years old

It's something that has been filtered through by my parents. I didn't know much about it, and they don't mind my not knowing much about it. They control the source of information—sort of like the high priest: you can't approach the altar too closely or you'll be struck dead. This purple heart in their background has become a justification for their present affluence. . . .

Hiram "Chub" Sherman, sixty years old, is an established Broadway actor.

It was rock-bottom living in New York then, it really was. Cars were left on the streets. There were no signs about restricted parking *(laughs)*. If somebody had a jal-

Photographer Dorothea Lange recorded this ironic scene in March, 1937, on a flat, bleak stretch of highway outside Los Angeles.

opy—a few friends, you know, would have some old car —it would sit there for months on end neither molested nor disturbed. It would just fall apart from old age.

You didn't count your possessions in terms of money in the bank. You counted on the fact that you had a row of empty milk bottles. Because those were cash, they could be turned in for a nickel deposit, and that would get you on the subway. If you took any stock in yourself, you looked to see how many milk bottles you had, because they counted. Two bottles: one could get you uptown, one could get you back. . . .

I remember being employed once to stand in front of St. Patrick's Cathedral on Fifth Avenue, Easter morning. With a clicker in each hand. A fashion woman had engaged me to note the acceptance of patent leather purses and white hats. Each white hat I saw, I clicked

my right hand. And each patent leather purse I saw, I clicked my left hand. Then I had to go home and tote up what the clickers said. White hats were in that spring, patent leather purses were out.

I remember also what you'd pick up odd dollars doing. There were sight-seeing buses—see Chinatown, see the Bowery, see New York. They were lined up right on Times Square. If you've ever noted a sight-seeing bus, there'll be a couple of people sitting on the bus. And they'd say: "It's leaving right away, guided tour, just leaving for the Bowery and Chinatown." Well, the people inside were usually shills. They're engaged for a quarter or fifty cents to sit there and look eager. I shilled in Times Square sight-seeing buses *(laughs)*. As people came on, you got off: "Excuse me for a moment." And then you got into another bus. It's a sitting job.

There were all sorts of things that went on like that from which you earned a living. It wasn't a very good living, but it kept you alive. . . .

Ben Isaacs, a salesman, now lives in a middle-class suburb.

We tried to struggle along living day by day. Then I couldn't pay the rent. I had a little car, but I couldn't pay no license for it. I left it parked against the court. I sold it for fifteen dollars in order to buy some food for the family. I had three little children. It was a time when I didn't even have money to buy a pack of cigarettes, and I was a smoker. I didn't have a nickel in my pocket.

Finally people started to talk me into going into the relief. . . . I didn't want to go on relief. Believe me, when I was forced to go to the office of the relief, the tears were running out of my eyes. I couldn't bear myself to take money from anybody for nothing. If it wasn't for those kids—I tell you the truth—many a time it came to my mind to go commit suicide. Then go ask for relief. But somebody has to take care of those kids. . . .

Wherever I went to get a job, I couldn't get no job. I went around selling razor blades and shoelaces. There was a day I would go over all the streets and come home with fifty cents, making a sale. That kept going until 1940, practically. Nineteen-thirty-nine the war started. Things started to get a little better. My wife found a job in a restaurant for twenty dollars a week. Right away, I sent a letter to the relief people: I don't think I would need their help any more. I was disgusted with relief, so ashamed. I couldn't face it any more.

Justin McCarthy quit college in 1933 and went to work in a Ford assembly plant near Chicago.

I sandpapered all the right-hand fenders. I was paid five dollars a day. . . . The gates were locked when you came in at eight o'clock in the morning. They weren't opened again until five o'clock in the evening. People brought their own lunch. No commissary wagons were permitted on the grounds. Nobody bothered to tell me. So I didn't eat that first day.

If you wanted to go to the toilet, you had to have permission of the foreman. He had to find a substitute for you on the assembly line who could sandpaper those two right fenders as they went by. If he couldn't right away, you held it *(laughs)*.

If you didn't punch that clock at eight o'clock, if you came in at two minutes past eight, you were docked one hour's pay. There wasn't any excuse. If you did this two or three times, you got fired.

I made the mistake of telling the foreman I had enrolled at Northwestern University night school. He said, "Mr. Ford isn't paying people to go to college. You're through."

General Robert E. Wood, who recently died, was a vice president of Sears Roebuck during the 1930's.

We had to lay off thousands of people. It was terrible. I used to go through the halls of the building and these little girls, they were all terrified. I remember one Italian girl I called in. She had a family of ten, father, mother, and eight children. She was the only one working. It was terrible. But we had to lay 'em off. I could see how frightened to death they were.

Tom Sutton, a lawyer, heads Operation Crescent, an organization of white property owners.

I remember standing in my father's office watching a march on City Hall. I was seven or eight. I remember his comment about red flags and revolution. He said, "The poor devils are just looking for bread." They weren't out to harm anyone. All they were marching for was food. I thought: Why were they looking for food? There were plenty of stores.

There was always talk in the house about the financial crisis. I remember listening to Father Coughlin about money-changers in the temple. I lived in a Protestant neighborhood. It seemed there were more Protestants listening to Father Coughlin than there were Catholics. My father listened to him. He was like everybody else: anybody that had a solution, they'd grab onto it.

He was a liberal and a Democrat and a strong supporter of Roosevelt. One of my favorite pastimes during the campaign was sitting across the front room watching him repeat after Roosevelt as Roosevelt talked. You know, telling off the other side. Since most of his brothers-in-law were conservative Republicans, he enjoyed that particularly.

I went along with him. I can remember writing a term paper in high school: "The Need for a Planned Economy." I take it out and read it once in a while, just to see how foolish youth can be.

Senator Russell Long talks about his father, Huey Long.

He was really catching on around the country. His plan was pretty well patterned after the old Populist philosophy. Money had gotten down to where a few people had practically all of it. He thought it was time you spread it among everybody. His share-the-wealth program was for one third of the nation's money to be divided among all the people, even though you did permit the other two thirds to be captured by the upper one per cent. It had a lot of popular appeal.

Seductive movie posters partially mask the blank faces of houses on an Atlanta street. The photograph was taken by Walker Evans.

His critics would say: in three or four years, the wealthy would have the money back in their coffers anyway. The Long people would answer: maybe so. But think what a good time we'd have in the meanwhile *(laughs)*.

Harry Hartman works in the bailiff's office in the Chicago County Building. He has been there for thirty-three years. His work deals with evictions, levies, and replevins (in which goods bought on credit are repossessed by the seller if the payments are not met).

We had 'em [replevins] every single day. We used to come there with trucks and take the food off the table. The husband would come runnin' out of the house. We'd have to put the food on the floor, take the tables

41

Some of the workers built shacks, some just spread their meager possessions on the ground in this migrant camp in Marysville, California. The photograph was taken by Dorothea Lange. Government-built compounds later replaced some of these pathetic settlements.

and chairs out. If they were real bad, we'd make arrangements, you understand, to leave a few things there or something. So they could get by. But it was pretty rough there for a lot of people.

Once we went to a house and there were three children. The table seemed to be part of the furniture company's inventory. That and the beds and some other things. The thing that struck us funny was that these people had almost the whole thing paid for when they went to the furniture company and bought something else. So instead of paying this and making a separate bill, the salesman said, "You take whatever you want and we'll put it on the original bill." They paid for that stuff, and then when they weren't able—when the Depression struck—to pay for the new articles they bought, everything was repossessed.

Mick Shufro was assistant director of the Chicago Housing Authority in the late 1930's.

A mother of nine children was receiving two quarts of milk. Because of a budgetary crisis, she was cut down to one quart. She raised hell at the relief station. She

became vituperative. The caseworker wrote her up as a psychotic. And sent her to a psychiatrist. Fortunately, he responded as few did at the time. He said: "When this woman stops reacting the way she does, let me know. Then she would be abnormal. . . ."

Elsa Ponselle, a young teacher during the Depression, is now the principal of one of Chicago's largest elementary schools.

At our school we had many Mexican children. When I get violent against big business, I think of those poor little kids. The Mexicans were imported to come up and work on the railroads, and when the work gave out, well, brother, can you spare a dime? They were thrust out, just like that. And they accepted it. I mean, this was the way the world was.

At times, when it was raining and snowing the middle-class children were all bundled up, or else kept at home. Our kids came to school every single day, whether they had anything to wear or not. 'Cause it was warm, the classroom was warm. . . .

Today the kids blithely make fifty dollars and off they

go and spend it. As they very properly should. One time somebody said to me, "What these kids need is to experience a depression." Two of us, remembering the hard times, screamed at him, "Never! Not in a thousand years!" I don't care how blithe they are in spending money. Nobody should experience a depression. No young person should. . . .

Pauline Kael is now the film critic of *The New Yorker* magazine.

When I attended Berkeley in 1936, so many of the kids had actually lost their fathers. They had wandered off in disgrace because they couldn't support their families. Other fathers had killed themselves so the family could have the insurance. Families had totally broken down. Each father took it as his personal failure. These middle-class men apparently had no social sense of what was going on, so they killed themselves.

It was still the Depression. There were kids who didn't have a place to sleep, huddling under bridges on the campus. I had a scholarship, but there were times when I didn't have food. The meals were often three candy bars. We lived communally and I remember feeding other kids by cooking up more spaghetti than I can ever consider again. . . .

Robert Havighurst is a professor at the Graduate School of Education, University of Chicago.

The S.D.S.-type of student was rather visible on the campus during the thirties. As I see it, I think they had more to object to than today's young dissenters. They emerged from the social soil of the Depression. They came from families where the father had no job, though desperately seeking one. No one living in that decade could avoid the feeling that something was terribly wrong with society. . . .

Clyde T. Ellis was in the Arkansas state senate from 1934 to 1938. He later was elected to Congress.

The Dirty Thirties—the phrase was coined where we had the dust storms. My people came from Arkansas, where the years of drought coincided with the hard years of the Depression. Even the one good year was no good. Everything dried . . . the springs, the wells, the ponds, the creeks, the rivers.

We saw bank failures everywhere. In my county, all but three failed. The president of the bank where my people had their little savings didn't wait to be indicted. He committed suicide. The worst thing we lost was hope. A man can endure a lot if he still has hope.

Mountain people are more rigorous than others. We lived a harder life. We had to grow or make most of the things we needed. The country never did lend itself to mechanization . . . still doesn't. Rock. We had relatives who just gave up. Broke up homes, scattered to different states. From down in my county, many would go to what we called DEtroit. Then they started to go to California, any way they could. Thumbing rides . . . I thumbed rides when I was peddling Bibles. It was during a summer, while still in high school. *The Grapes of Wrath* was no exaggeration. We saw it, we lived it. The Joad family had an automobile. We never could afford one. Had we been able to, I'm sure my family would have done the same—gone to California. And we were better off than most. . . .

Ruth Loriks lives on a farm in Arlington, South Dakota. Her husband, Emil, was a state senator from 1927 to 1934.

This neighbor woman lost her husband and, of course, he was owing in the bank. So the auctioneers come out there, and she served lunch, and she stood weeping in the windows. "There goes our last cow. . . ." And the horses. She called 'em by names. It just pretty near broke our hearts. They didn't give her a chance to take care of her bills. They never gave her an offer. They just came out and cleared it out. She just stood there crying. . . .

Oscar Heline, seventy-eight years old, has lived on the same Iowa farm all his life.

What I remember most of those times is that poverty creates desperation and desperation creates violence. In Plymouth County—Le Mars—just west of us, a group met one morning and decided they were going to stop the judge from issuing any more deficiency judgments. This judge had a habit of very quickly okaying foreclosure sales. These farmers couldn't stand it any more. They'd see their neighbors sold out.

There were a few judges who would refuse to take the cases. They'd postpone it or turn it over to somebody else. But this one was pretty gruff and arrogant: you do this, you do that, it's my court. When a bunch of farmers are going broke every day and the judge sits there very proudly and says: this is my court . . . they say: who the hell are you? He was just a fellow human being, same as they were.

These farmers gathered this one particular day. I suppose some of 'em decided to have a little drink, and so they developed a little courage. They decided: we'll go down and teach that judge a lesson. They marched into the courtroom, hats on, demanded to visit with him. *He* decided he would teach *them* a lesson. So he says: "Gentlemen, this is my court. Remove your hats and address the court properly."

They just laughed at him. They said, "We're not concerned whose court this is. We came here to get redress from your actions. The things you're doing, we can't stand to have done to us any more." The argument kept on, and got rougher. He wouldn't listen. He threatened them. So they drug him from his chair, pulled him down the steps of the courthouse, and shook a rope in front of his face. Then, tarred and feathered him.

The governor called out the National Guard. And put these farmers behind barbed wire. Just imagine *(he weeps)* . . . in this state. You don't forget these things.

Emil Loriks

There's a saying: Depressions are farm led and farm fed. That was true in the thirties. As farmers lost their purchasing power, the big tractors piled up at the Minneapolis-Moline plant in the Twin Cities. One day they closed their doors and turned their employees out to beg or starve. My cousin was one of them. I took my truck to Minneapolis and brought him and his family out to my farm for the duration. They stayed with us until the company opened up again, two or three years later.

During my first session in the state senate, in 1927, five hundred farmers came marching up Capitol Hill. It thrilled me. I didn't know farmers were intelligent enough to organize *(laughs)*. They stayed there for two days. It was a strength I didn't realize we had.

The day after they left, a senator got up and attacked them as anarchists and bolsheviks *(laughs)*. They had a banner, he said, redder than anything in Moscow, Russia. What was this banner? It was a piece of muslin, hung up in the auditorium. It said: "We Buy Together, We Sell Together, We Vote Together." This was the radical danger *(laughs)*. They'd been building co-operatives, which the farmers badly needed.

Horace Cayton, a Negro, is a sociologist and writer.

What was the black people's attitude toward Roosevelt?

Oh yeah, that was something. He broke the tradition. My father told me: "The Republicans are the ship. All else is the sea." Frederick Douglass said that. They didn't go for Roosevelt much in '32. But the W.P.A. came along and Roosevelt came to be a god. It was really great. You worked, you got a paycheck, and you had some dignity. Even when a man raked leaves, he got paid, he had some dignity. All the songs they used to have about W.P.A.: Oh, I'm for you, Mr. President / I'm for you all the way / You can take away the alphabet / But don't take away this W.P.A.

When they got on W.P.A., you know what they'd mostly do. First, they'd buy some clothes. And tried to get a little better place to live. The third thing was to

get your teeth fixed. When you're poor, you let your teeth go. Especially the child. If she's got a rotten or snaggle tooth and that tooth may ache, dulled by aspirin or something or whisky. Then they'd pull them out. They'd get their teeth fixed. W.P.A. . . .

Ed Paulsen did odd jobs in the 1930's. Now he has an administrative job with UNICEF.

The N.Y.A. [National Youth Administration] was my salvation. I could just as easily have been in Sing Sing as with the U.N. Every bit as good a chance. Hell, yes. Everybody was a criminal. You stole, you cheated through. You were getting by, survival. Stole clothes off lines, stole milk off back porches, you stole bread. I remember going through Tucumcari, New Mexico, on a freight. We made a brief stop. There was a grocery store, a supermarket kind of thing for those days. I beat it off the train and came back with rolls and crackers. This guy is standing in the window shaking his fist at you.

It wasn't a big thing, but it created a coyote mentality. You were a predator. You had to be. We were coyotes in the thirties, the jobless.

No, I don't see the Depression as an ennobling experience.

Daisy Singer is a photographer who grew up in New York.

We lived on Park Avenue before the Depression, like in eleven or fourteen rooms. One of those big apartments which are essentially very dreary. But they're what people hoped to achieve. After the crash, we moved to Central Park West, which wasn't such a terrible comedown. Except my grandparents moved in with us: keep up appearances and double in brass.

I remember vaguely family conferences, which took place behind closed doors. Like loans negotiated and things like that. The front would have to be maintained because I've learned that in business if people smell failure in you, you've had it. . . .

I always had governesses. I remember going to the park with the one I really liked. There was a shantytown. Like a Hooverville. It was for me the palpable memory of the other side of the tracks. Ever since, when I encounter poverty, it is this memory . . . holding the hand of one's governess. For years, I felt exempt. I grew up feeling immune and exempt from circumstance. One of the things I suffered from was that I never felt adversity. I was confirmed in a sense of unreality. I never saw a real bread line. I saw it in the movies.

We never went far afield. Once, I remember, my brother was robbed. He was twelve, so that was about three years after the crash. The outside world was so far from us, one didn't expect to encounter it. The doors were shut, as if there were some kind of contagion out there. I guess it was innocence, but I don't think of it as anything pretty at all. . . .

Virginia Durr is a member of an old Alabama family. Her husband was with the Federal Communications Commission during F.D.R.'s administration.

Oh, no, the Depression was not a romantic time. It was a time of terrible suffering. The contradictions were so obvious that it didn't take a very bright person to realize something was terribly wrong.

Have you ever seen a child with rickets? Shaking as with palsy. No proteins, no milk. And the companies pouring milk into gutters. People with nothing to wear and they were plowing up cotton. People with nothing to eat and they killed the pigs. If that wasn't the craziest system in the world, could you imagine anything more idiotic? This was just insane.

And people blamed themselves, not the system. They felt they had been at fault: "If we hadn't bought that old radio". . . "if we hadn't bought that old second-hand car." Among the things that horrified me were the preachers—the fundamentalists. They would tell the people they suffered because of their sins. And the people believed it. God was punishing them. Their children were starving because of their sins. . . .

Tom, twenty-one, is the son of a very successful businessman. He is now in Canada, in defiance of his 1-A draft status.

My father talks about the Depression didactically. He tries to draw little lessons from it. He has an anecdote every time the subject comes up. It's sort of a heroic past for him. It makes him an extremist: you have one analysis you can fit everything into. He has an extremist definition of what the goal of a nation should be . . . what a guy should be preparing for at school. Since most people feel this way, it's not called extreme. But it is. . . .

My father is slick. He tries to say something we will dig. The other night we played Billie Holiday, and he started naming some of her other songs. You see, he's really saying, "I am one of you." He uses the same sort of mechanism at work.

He's become a king in welfare capitalism, because he knows how to work with labor. He's always said that unions are the greatest. I'm sure he was a real slick worker when they were changing their roles from real unions to company-minded unions. Which they are today. He learned all this in the Depression. It was his war.

Peggy Terry, again

. . . It's different today. People are made to feel ashamed now if they don't have anything. Back then, I'm not sure how the rich felt. I think the rich were as contemptuous of the poor then as they are now. But among the people that I knew, we all had an understanding that it wasn't our fault. It was something that had happened to the machinery. Most people blamed Hoover, and they cussed him up one side and down the other . . . it was all his fault. I'm not saying he's blameless, but I'm not saying either it was all his fault. Our system doesn't run by just one man and it doesn't fall by just one man, either.

When I read *Grapes of Wrath*, that was like reliving my life. Particularly the part where they lived in this government camp. Because when we were picking fruit in Texas, we lived in a government place like that. They came around and they helped the women make mattresses. See, we didn't have anything. And they showed us how to sew and make dresses. And every Saturday night, we'd have a dance. And when I was reading *Grapes of Wrath*, this was just like my life. I was never so proud of poor people before, as I was after I read that book.

Jack, twenty years old

A Depression might be interesting today. It could *really* be something. To be on the bum, and have nobody say: "Look, I'll give you ten thousand dollars if you'd just come back and go to school." We have a choice today. What would it be like if we had no choice?

In this photograph by Arthur Rothstein an unemployed man, his belongings lashed to his car, heads hopefully for Oregon.

45

*The notorious financier's properties included railroads, yachts,
and newspapers, but none was more precious to him
than Lyndhurst, the family castle on the Hudson. It would have
distressed him to know that it now belongs to you and me*

THE REALMS OF GOULD

By FRANK KINTREA

In the summer of 1841 Philip Hone, the New York merchant and politician whose diary has
been such a rich mine of illuminating comment upon his contemporaries, "went on another
pleasant excursion up the [Hudson] valley to Tarrytown. . . ." One of the sights of that idyllic
countryside to inspire his diaristic pen was the new country villa of his old political rival,
General William Paulding.

"In the course of our drive we went to see Mr. Paulding's magnificent house, yet unfin-
ished, on the bank below Tarrytown. It is an immense edifice of white or gray marble, resem-
bling a baronial castle, or rather a Gothic monastery, with towers, turrets and trellises; archways, armories and airholes; peaked windows and pinnacled roofs, and many other fantastics
too tedious to enumerate, the whole constituting an edifice of gigantic size, with no room in it;
which if I mistake not, will one of these days be designated as 'Paulding's folly'. . . ."

Throughout the ages men have been given to erecting monuments of unsuitable grandeur
to their own glory. In the nineteenth century the banks of the lordly Hudson were especially
conducive to the construction of a host of inappropriately palatial or uniquely fantastic dwellings. Unlike the enormous "cottages" that erupted at Newport and other fashionable resorts
near the close of the century, when ostentatious display had become an essential ingredient of
social rank, the large houses of the Hudson Valley were the products of a more romantic and
idealistic spirit. Many were buried in remote fastnesses where only eagles and hawks could be
impressed by their grandeur. In the dreamy vale of the mists enshrouding the great river,
inspired by long attachment to the forts, castles, and other trappings of feudal ancestors and
by a deep sense of insecurity here on earth, many men were tempted to build their "castles in
the sand" of stone and mortar.

Mr. Hone's dire prophecy did not come true. Unlike other architectural excrescences that
mushroomed over the American landscape in the nineteenth century, General Paulding's
"immense edifice" never became a derelict monument to the folly of man's pride and vanity.
Lyndhurst, as it was christened by a later owner, still stands, recognized by connoisseurs of
architecture as "one of the great houses of America . . . uniting in its walls the beginning and
the culmination of Hudson River Gothic."

For the social historian, the men and women who have lived at Lyndhurst provide a superb
epitome of the growth of the American economy in the nineteenth century and an unglossed
portrait gallery of those who have been both its leaders and often its choicest benefici-
aries. General Paulding was a rich lawyer who married an heiress of the Rhinelander family

*Jay Gould looked like this about the time—in 1880—that he acquired Lyndhurst. The great baronial hall
has here been transposed to its master's lap by a bit of artful dodging on the part of our art director.*

richer than himself. George Merritt, who bought Lynd-hurst from Paulding's descendants in 1864, was first a prosperous merchant and later a successful investor in the booming industrial by-products of the tremendous growth of railroads in the eighteen-fifties and sixties. But the Pauldings and Merritts have long been forgotten, and Lyndhurst itself would have shared their fate if one of the greatest of the robber barons who dominated the American economy in the last quarter of the nineteenth century had not rescued it from oblivion. For more than eighty of the 130 years of its existence Lyndhurst was the home of a family whose name still bears a sinister fame in the annals of American business and finance.

In a land where costly and substantial structures are built and demolished with more reckless abandon than ever before in the history of the world, it is a miracle that so many of America's great houses have been able to survive the ravages of death, taxes, and social change to which they are a natural prey. Without roots in a still-functioning landed aristocracy, once the fortune that gave them life is scattered their existence becomes a series of crises, each greater than the one before.

The last and most crucial period in Lyndhurst's own struggle for survival began far away in Paris on November 29, 1961, with the death of a sad old lady who had long outlived her time. Anna, Duchesse de Talleyrand-Périgord, was dead at the age of eighty-six. Though her name and her exalted title, dating back to the twelfth century in France, meant nothing to most Americans, the obituary accounts of her fairy-tale life stirred memories of an éra in our past that still haunts us. The Duchesse, long ago, before the turn of the century, had been plain Anna Gould. She was the last of the six children of Jay Gould and the last mistress of Lyndhurst.

In 1838, when General Paulding was building Lynd-hurst, Jay Gould was an infant, two years old, growing up on a small hillside farm in the Catskills near Roxbury, New York, where his parents struggled to make a decent living. The Goulds were proud, respectable folk of old New England stock, but in that day, when only the rags of the rags-to-riches tradition were yet evident, they would never have dared to dream that a son of theirs could cross the immense gulf of wealth and social position between themselves and the Pauldings. Yet forty-two years later, in 1880, when Jay Gould bought Lyndhurst as casually as most men buy a pair of shoes, his swift rise from humble beginnings to wealth and power had already become a familiar story that any ambitious young man could at least hope to emulate.

The Goulds first came to Lyndhurst in the summer of 1878, when they leased it for the season from Mr. Merritt's widow. The year before had been one of the darker and more turbulent years in what now seems that long and complacent era of supposedly inevitable cycles of boom or bust from which the American economy did not emerge until after the Great Depression of the 1930's. A majority of the hastily built and overexpanded railroads were in bankruptcy, and two thirds of the iron mills lay idle. Workers and their families were starving and destitute. Despair and misery bred anarchists and agitators, violence and bloodshed. But for Jay Gould, the cool and crafty market operator, it was a year of immensely profitable short sales and a feast of securities bought at bargain prices. It was also, for one who took a wry pride in acknowledging himself to be "the most hated man in America," a time of physical danger and of fear for the safety of his family. Lyndhurst, with its thick marble walls, its turrets and battlements, had a comforting air of impregnable security—especially after Gould realistically reinforced it with an around-the-clock patrol of armed guards.

There was no market for Lyndhurst in 1878. The new crop of parvenus preferred to build new houses in a more opulent style, with better plumbing. Socially, the lower Hudson Valley was becoming a stagnant backwater for the less fashionable. Mr. Merritt, in his brief reign, had expanded Lyndhurst beyond the needs of his widow and children. Like the overextended railroads upon which Gould preyed, it was another bargain to be devoured. In 1880 Jay Gould acquired full title to Lyndhurst and its broad domain of 550 acres for what even then was the rather miserable sum of $250,000.

Lyndhurst was a happy choice for the Goulds. As important as security from cranks and embittered speculators was the security it gave Mrs. Gould and the children from the snubs and rebuffs of the New York elite, and the even less palatable disdain of dedicated social climbers, to all of which Gould himself was impervious. His personal indifference to social aspiration undoubtedly added to the suspicion and distrust with which he has always been regarded. Mrs. Gould's own modest social ambitions were at least partially mollified by invitations to the tea parties and garden fetes of the local aristocracy. For the children—George Jay, sixteen; Edwin, fourteen; Helen, twelve; Howard, nine; Anna, five; and Frank Jay, three—Lyndhurst was a fairy-tale castle of endless delights. For their father it was a haven from the jungles of finance, where he could find the solitude he seemed to crave, tending his beloved orchids or brooding over his books. As his daughter Helen said years later, "He was a terribly silent man . . ." and the Gothic shadows of Lyndhurst suited him well.

The years from 1880 to 1886 were good years for the Goulds and for Lyndhurst. Gould was no longer a mere stock-market operator. After titanic struggles he had gained operating control of the entire elevated railway system of New York City and of the Western Union

Telegraph Company, and had become the overlord of nearly ten thousand miles of railroad right of way. Jay Gould was one of the richest and most powerful men in the world, and one of the most unobtrusive. Life at Lyndhurst did not change. Mr. Gould commuted to work on his steam yacht, *Atalanta*, one of his few luxuries, with neighbors such as Cyrus Field or Chauncey Depew occasionally hitching a ride. Mrs. Gould had her domestic duties and her garden club affairs, but there were few notable social occasions at Lyndhurst. It was the children who were the life of the house during these happy years, and if they had been able to foresee the future, they might have wished to stay young forever in their enchanted castle. It may be that the Lyndhursts of this world are really meant only for children of all ages who never grow up. But, in the early evening of September 14, 1886, whatever magic spell Lyndhurst possessed for the Goulds was broken by one of those events that now seem absurd but that were catastrophic to family life in the Victorian era.

The following morning the *New York Times* devoted the place of honor on its front page to what its headlines described as "A QUIET CEREMONY IN THE PATERNAL HALL AT IRVINGTON, AND NONE BUT RELATIVES PRESENT." The quiet ceremony was the marriage of George Jay Gould, now twenty-two, pride of his father and idol of his mother, to Miss Edith Kingdon of Brooklyn. The paternal hall was Lyndhurst. Miss Kingdon, from all accounts, was an eminently respectable young lady, but, alas, she was an actress, and Mrs. Gould would never recover from the shock. For weeks afterward, she would break into fits of weeping. "Oh Alice, why has this happened," she would sob, a niece who was present on one of these mournful occasions remembered. "Just to think of it, George married to an actress! What next? How do we know that Helen won't fall in love with a coachman?"

There was not the remotest danger that Helen, then a shy, prim, and inflexibly pious girl of eighteen, would ever fall in love with a coachman, although in 1886 coachmen were considered nearly as great a menace to wealthy young virgins as actresses were to young gentlemen. When her mother died on January 13, 1889, at the age of fifty-one, following a series of strokes, Helen was ready to take over as mistress of Lyndhurst. It was not an easy role to fill. In addition to Lyndhurst, there was the town house at 579 Fifth Avenue to be looked after; the two younger children, Anna and Frank, had still to be raised; and her father, to whom Helen was fanatically devoted and who was now mortally ill of tuberculosis, needed her constant care. But the young lady of nineteen, now more prim and more pious than ever, who would be famous for nearly a quarter of a century as the militantly virtuous Miss Gould, was ideally cast for the

CONTINUED ON PAGE 54

Lyndhurst was an early design of Alexander Jackson Davis, who became famous as an exponent of the Gothic Revival style in university and public buildings. Below: the ultimate in pigeonhole desks, in Lyndhurst's "office room," together with such objets d'art *as a picture of Gould's yacht, the* Atalanta, *and a spittoon.*

BOTH: PAULUS LEESER

The architect of Lyndhurst, Alexander Jackson Davis, was the most versatile, prolific, and influential practitioner of his day. The first two owners of the mansion faithfully relied on his judgment while the building was growing. "Make designs for all the windows of the library . . ." Paulding wrote him in 1841. "Rich colors will tell well in the small window above the big one . . . Here expense may be excused. The big window must be a nonpareil ... I leave this entirely to your taste." About a quarter of a century later the next owner, George Merritt, commissioned Davis to design a new wing in the same Gothic Revival style as the original structure. At that time the library (above) was converted into an art gallery to house Merritt's collection of paintings. The chairs silhouetted against the windows follow designs made by Davis for Paulding; those in the foreground came from Gould's yacht.

The entire suite of furniture designed for the new dining room (above) when Lyndhurst was enlarged in the 1860's has remained in the house ever since. Like the bulk of the early furnishings, the tables and chairs are picturesque evocations of medieval designs. A number of Davis' original drawings for such forms, as well as for the house itself, have been preserved. His prestige as a tastemaker is evident in the notes his patrons sent him. At one point during the construction of the original building, Paulding asked the architect to check on some mantels he had designed before they were delivered for installation. "If you see anything offensive . . . put your veto on it. They are extremely elegant and I wish them to be correct examples of the style. How the ladies will dote on them." Merritt employed Davis' services in the same spirit, and with similar respect Jay Gould made no significant alterations in Lyndhurst's style.

Although the Goulds did not essentially alter the fabric of Lynd-hurst, they did introduce furnishings that reflect the changing and eclectic fashions of later years and the personal interests of the later owners. In the Duchesse's guest bedroom, shown above, the original architectural framework is intact—the painted, rib-vaulted ceiling, the window embrasure with its pointed-arch moldings, the mul-lioned casements, and the colorful lunette remain as Davis planned them. But everything displayed against that highly stylized back-ground bespeaks a newer spirit. On the French desk shown in the right foreground are, among other things, a Tiffany lamp that was a wedding gift to Helen Gould, a painted brass inkwell in the shape of an Egyptian head, and a porcelain bowl. In the far corner, a Chinese lacquer screen hides the radiator. On the night table beside the Gothic bed is a photograph of one of the Duchesse's sons.

When the house was enlarged by Merritt, the old dining room became the new library (above). The present furnishings of the room are in a mixture of styles of various periods. Prominently shown in the foreground is a relic of Jay Gould's first business enterprise: an odometer he used as a young surveyor. The unusual armchair at dead center of the illustration was made at New York in 1869 by George Hunzinger, a fashionable immigrant craftsman of the period. However, amid such later accretions, the massive bookcases and the great armchair shown at the left, echoing the unchanged Gothic style of the interior architecture, are strong reminders of Davis' original genius. He not only supplied the plans for the room and its furnishings; he also gave Merritt a list of books appropriate for such a library. In sum, he created at Lyndhurst what is today considered the finest example of the Gothic Revival style in America.

part of the daughter who stays home to take the place of her mother and who becomes in time the doting aunt of her brothers' and sister's ungrateful children.

George, in spite of a fondness for the haunts of a young man about town, had gone to work at seventeen, and Edwin had made his first million in the stock market soon after dropping out of Columbia College. At an age when most of their second-generation contemporaries were drifting into the life of confirmed gentlemen of leisure, both were able and hard-working railroad men. They took over the management of most of their father's complex affairs, but his feverish mind would not permit him to seek the rest that might have prolonged his life. He still commuted back and forth to the city on the *Atalanta* and plotted the fulfillment of his great dream of a Gould system extending from coast to coast. If he had lived longer, it is quite likely that he would have succeeded.

Jay Gould died on December 2, 1892, at the age of fifty-six, in his ugly brownstone mansion on the northeast corner of Fifth Avenue at Forty-seventh Street. He was no more popular dead than alive. Aside from the pious platitudes of acquaintances and camp followers, there was little public lament. The *New York Times*, in an editorial sternly deploring his career, did pay him one tribute he would have liked. Jay Gould, the *Times* said, "never gave himself the trouble of making any false pretenses." His family was stricken with a deep and lasting grief, and his few close friends were saddened by the passing of a remarkable man. Lyndhurst, with crepe on its great doors and its flags at half-mast, mourned the death of a kind and considerate master and faced its own future with trepidation.

The estate of Jay Gould was officially appraised at

Gould children, naturally, grew up in lavish surroundings and were equipped with costly playthings. At left above, Helen, Edwin, Howard, and Frank pose (with two friends, seated) in Fourth of July array about 1885. Above: George Jay Gould's children—Kingdon, Marjorie, Edith, Jay, and Vivian—surround the chauffeur in toy cars which had real engines (1902).

$84,309,258, exclusive of Louisiana timber lands which, in accord with the laws of that state, passed directly to his heirs, and from which some twelve million dollars was eventually realized. Up to that time, it had been exceeded only by the estates of Commodore Vanderbilt and his son William Henry, but the will disposing of it was a relatively simple document. There were no bequests outside the family, and even the one-thousand-dollar token remembrances to friends and business associates, which he had directed in a curious surge of death-bed sentimentality, were later disallowed by the courts and removed from the pockets of his executors, who had dutifully paid them.

Contrary to the prevailing pattern of testamentary distributions among the rich in the nineteenth century, when Astors and Vanderbilts and their imitators were seeking to concentrate their wealth in the hands of their eldest or ablest sons, Jay Gould treated his children rather equally. The money left after the payments of debts, taxes, and administration expenses was divided into six trust funds, each valued at approximately $12,500,000. Each of his four sons and two daughters received the income for life from one of these trusts, with the principal to be distributed among their issue when they died.

The Fifth Avenue mansion, valued at four hundred thousand dollars, was bequeathed outright to Helen. Lyndhurst, however, was left in a state of testamentary limbo. Until Frank came of age, Helen was given the use of it, free of taxes, plus six thousand dollars a month, in the expectation that Anna, Frank, and perhaps even Howard would make their home with her; after that it would become a disposable part of the estate. Howard, of course, at the age of twenty-two, could not be relied upon. He came and went as he pleased and, to Helen's utter dismay, was already showing a decided preference for ladies of the lighter stage.

On December 4, 1898, Frank Jay Gould celebrated his twenty-first birthday by collecting some $3,500,000 in cash and securities in payment of the income that had been accumulating in the trust for his benefit since his father's death in 1892. On the same day, Lyndhurst became a minor and somewhat bothersome asset of the estate. Valued at six hundred thousand dollars in the transfer tax appraisal, it now fell into the same unproductive category as the mausoleum at Woodlawn Cemetery and the *Atalanta*, each valued at one hundred thousand dollars. Lyndhurst and the *Atalanta* were not only unproductive; they were costly to maintain, and it was the duty of the executors to dispose of them as quickly as possible.

For months the fate of Lyndhurst was uncertain. To Helen it was a sacred trust to which they all owed allegiance; as a tribute to the memory of their father and mother, it must remain in the family forever. But the family unity that Jay Gould had hoped to establish by the equal division of his fortune had already been seriously disrupted by frictions arising from George's arro-

gant usurpation of the major titles and perquisites of the Goulds' far-flung empire. George himself, although he was the eldest son, was not interested in Lyndhurst. He and Edith, in their campaign for social acceptance, were already enthroned at Georgian Court, in Lakewood, New Jersey, then described as the most magnificent country estate in America. Edwin, Howard, Frank, and Anna had grandiose housing plans of their own, and Helen was desolated to learn that there was no lawful way in which Lyndhurst could remain on the books of the estate with her in possession.

Early in 1899 Helen moved out of Lyndhurst—at least officially. Actually, legal guardians for infant remaindermen of the trust funds would later claim that she had never given up possession, and that expenses for which she was liable had been improperly charged to the principal of the estate. It is a fact that during the period from January to August of 1899, when Lyndhurst was supposedly vacant, its maintenance cost the estate over sixteen thousand dollars. This included wages for gardeners, farmhands, a coachman, and a groom, and feed for horses, cows, and dogs. Even when inflated into the depreciated dollars of 1970, this outlay now seems hardly commensurate with the grandeur of Lyndhurst and the wealth of the Goulds. Nevertheless, although there was no gush of money going down the drain, Lyndhurst was the steady drip of a leaky faucet, and its retention by the estate would have been a fiduciary dereliction that even trustees as notably lax as George, Edwin, Helen, and Howard Gould could not countenance.

Fortunately for Lyndhurst, however, Helen was obsessed by a dread of parting with anything her father had ever owned or used, be it nondividend-paying stock in one of the rickety tributary roads of the Gould system or an unfashionable neo-Gothic mansion in a socially declining neighborhood. As long as she lived, she would never permit anyone but herself to sleep in his bed. No stranger would occupy Lyndhurst: she would buy it herself.

The traumatic experience she must have undergone while its fate was being debated was revealed years later when she appeared before a referee appointed by the Supreme Court of New York to defend her acts as a co-trustee of her father's estate. Under cross-examination she became almost hysterical in refusing to answer questions regarding her alleged improper occupancy of Lyndhurst after Frank became twenty-one, and legal eyebrows were raised by her unshakable insistence that she had not the faintest idea of what she had paid for it. Yet, incredible though it may seem to most of us, it is not altogether impossible that a lady with an income ranging between five and seven hundred thousand dollars a year, when income taxes were still only a faint cloud on the horizon, may have been unable to recall what she had paid for a house. It had been a complicated and somewhat bitter transaction extending over nearly six years, from the time she made a down payment of one hundred thousand dollars in 1899, before a definite price had been agreed upon, until she made a final payment of $37,585.41 on February 3, 1905. In the interim she had paid off five interest-bearing notes amounting to $244,847.41, for a total payment of $382,432.82.

Although Edwin Gould testified that the price was an average of appraisals made by three qualified realtors, several of the crusty guardians at law of her numerous nephews and nieces did not think that it was enough. For Helen Gould, whatever the price she had paid for Lyndhurst, it was exactly that much more than she had wanted to pay or that she felt she should have paid. In the unlikely event that she ever questioned the infallibility of her father, it would have to have been because he had not left Lyndhurst to her outright.

Helen Gould reigned as absolute queen of Lyndhurst for over forty years. Early in her career as *the* Miss Gould she won national acclaim as the ardent patroness of innumerable morally uplifting and worthy causes. For many years, according to family tradition, she gave away more than half of her income. In private, constantly attended by a retinue of female relatives, friends, and servants, she lived in an almost perpetual state of shock and maidenly confusion over the disastrous marriages and scandalous affairs of Howard and Frank. But she still took a childish delight in private-car inspection trips of Gould railroads and in the homage of operating officials who rolled out the red carpet to greet her along the way.

At the age of forty-four, Miss Gould, the quaint little lady in the dowdy clothes who was the image of the rich spinster aunt everyone dreams of having, shocked the nation by announcing her engagement to Finley J. Shepard, a minor operating official in the Gould System. They were married at Lyndhurst on January 22, 1913, a holy day in the bride's calendar because it was the fiftieth anniversary of the wedding of her mother and father. It was one of the great days in the history of Lyndhurst. A special train brought guests from New York, flags were flown by the people in Irvington, and the old house was filled with flowers and excitement. Mr. Shepard was a handsome, stalwart figure in the best tradition of the Young Men's Christian Association, whose tastes rather miraculously coincided with those of his bride. They spent their honeymoon at Lyndhurst.

It was a happy marriage for the Shepards as they moved back and forth with the seasons between 579 Fifth Avenue in the winter, the old Gould homestead at Roxbury for the summer, and Lyndhurst in the spring and fall. And it was a happy marriage for Lyndhurst, for the clatter of growing children again resounded in its halls. Mrs. Shepard could not bear children of her own,

but she and her husband adopted three orphans—two girls and a boy—and raised another boy as a foster child. Frank Gould's two girls by his first marriage frequently spent the nine months of each year allotted to him with their Aunt Helen. Much to her distress, however, although the smart but immodest little frocks in which they arrived were promptly banished in favor of voluminous pinafores, nine months were hopelessly inadequate to undo the sophistication acquired in the three months spent with their mother. When they were all at Lyndhurst together, with their entourage of nurses, governesses, and maids, it was a crowded, busy household that justified Hone's description of Lyndhurst as "an edifice of gigantic size, with no room in it."

For people of wealth, the Shepards had little taste for lavish display and in their later years preferred the simpler life at Roxbury, where the old Gould house had been remodelled and enlarged so as to accommodate their extensive ménage. In honor of its new dignity it was given a name of its own. Not unexpectedly, in view of its proximity to the Jay Gould Memorial Reformed Church, which the children had erected soon after their father's death, it was called Kirkside. Lyndhurst, while never neglected, entered a state of decline matching that of its mistress after she suffered a stroke in the fall of 1932. As the cozy realm of sanctimonious piety and of reverence for the rich simply because they were rich, in which she had flourished, was engulfed in the stock market crash of 1929 and the Great Depression of the 1930's, the once dauntless Miss Gould became a quaint and somewhat irrational little old lady. The diminishing income from her trust perplexed and alarmed her. The New Deal infuriated her. The twin menaces of atheism and communism, inseparably linked in her mind in a

In this Judge *cartoon of 1889 Ward McAllister, New York's social arbiter, offers a tray of European titles to nubile American heiresses. One of Jay Gould's daughters and a granddaughter— see pages 62–63—were destined to marry titled foreigners.*

conspiracy lurking under every bed, terrified her. Even the girls at Vassar, she was convinced, had become so irreligious and so dangerously radical that she withdrew several scholarship grants.

Helen Gould Shepard died at Roxbury on December 21, 1938, at the age of seventy, in the house where her father had been born. In her last will and testament she bequeathed the Fifth Avenue mansion and Kirkside to "my beloved husband," but surprisingly Lyndhurst was passed over in silence to become another of the anonymous assets comprising her residuary estate. The net value of the entire estate, according to the transfer tax appraisal, was $3,272,918. Mr. Shepard, as the residuary legatee, inherited most of it. Sadly, however, since Mrs. Shepard had had no children of her own, the far larger amount constituting the principal of her trust fund was distributed among Howard, Anna, Frank, and the surviving children of George and Edwin, who had died earlier. In accord with the terms of her father's will, her adopted orphans were firmly excluded.

Lyndhurst, to the prudent Mr. Shepard, was merely a wasting asset devouring his capital, and he was anxious to be rid of it as quickly as possible. In 1939, even more than in 1880, the market for a Lyndhurst was negligible. Even the rich were still suffering from the Great Depression: income taxes were becoming genuinely burdensome, and fears aroused by F. D. R. and the New Deal still lingered. The abundant supply of servants and other menials at low wages, so vital to the flourishing existence of great houses, was being eroded by social change. The Goulds themselves were Lyndhurst's best and perhaps only hope of survival.

Of the six children of Jay Gould who had grown up at Lyndhurst, George, Edwin, and now Helen were dead. Of the living, Howard had deserted a grandiose folly on Long Island, liberally emblazoned with what he fondly believed to be the Gould coat of arms and unblushingly called Castle Gould, and was now settled permanently into the life of an English country gentleman. Frank Jay had lived in France, where he had extensive business interests and grand personal establishments, for over a quarter of a century. In addition, he owned a twenty-seven-room Tudor mansion a few miles down the road from Lyndhurst, near Ardsley. He had bought it in 1933, but he had never lived in it, and so far as is known, he may never have bothered even to look at it. Eventually, he gave it away. Anna, once the little girl who had played with her dolls at Lyndhurst, was now the Duchesse de Talleyrand, mistress of palaces and chateaux in France, where she had lived ever since her marriage forty-four years before to a charming rogue named Count Boni de Castellane.

The market for European titles in exchange for American heiresses and dollars, which flourished in the last quarter of the nineteenth century, had reached its peak in 1895 when a reluctant Consuelo Vanderbilt, at the insistence of a mother who felt that American males could no longer be deemed eligible for the hand of a Vanderbilt, became the Duchess of Marlborough. To a public unaware of such social nuances, the marriage of Anna Gould to Count Boni de Castellane on March 4 of that same year was an almost equally astounding event. But Anna, unlike Miss Vanderbilt, was an eager and happy victim of her own romantic daydreams. Boni himself may not have been so happy. Penniless though he was, the antenuptual agreements had been a rude shock to his vanity. Not only the principal of the trust fund but the income it produced, thanks to Jay Gould's testamentary wariness, were beyond his grasp. But Anna loved him, and he was confident that once back in France, free from the scrutiny of Helen (who had distrusted him on sight), he could teach his unsophisticated bride the art of spending her great income as elegantly and as lavishly as if it were his own.

Boni was an expensive luxury even for Anna Gould. Her income of five to seven hundred thousand pre-income-tax dollars a year, when she and Boni were cutting a wide swath through the Paris of *la belle époque*, was not up to his extravagant taste in pink marble palaces filled with old masters and objets d'art and his fondness for entertaining on a grand scale. When he became surfeited with costly possessions and bored by the domestic felicities of a wife and children, gambling and women provided equally extravagant substitutes. Before Anna finally managed to escape to America with their three sons in 1906 and to divorce him for his flagrant affairs with other women, it has been conservatively estimated that he squandered five to six million dollars of her money in a monumental binge of supercilious elegance and frivolity. In justice to Boni it should be said that, until he slipped on what he blithely described as "the orange peel" of various sentimental adventures, Anna was a willing accomplice who constantly reproached George and Helen for not providing her with more dollars to squander. Oddly enough, she was the first to criticize George for his imprudent and, as it later proved, improper use of estate funds to shore up the Gould railroads, and she was furious with him for permitting a sizable portion of her income to be mortgaged for years to pay off the swarms of French tradesmen who had unctuously overextended credit to Boni and his American heiress. In spite of it all, Anna's financial difficulties eventually faded into the past as her share of the estate continued to produce a magic flow of American dollars. During the period of sixty-eight years from 1893 until her death in 1961 nearly thirty-five million dollars in income, plus some four millions from principal of the trusts for Helen and Howard when they died without issue of their own, was either paid to her directly by the trustees or was withheld to pay her debts and taxes.

After divorcing Boni, Anna, by now addicted to titles, married his cousin, Elie, Duc de Talleyrand-Périgord. The Duc, while he did not frown on American dollars, was the possessor of vast family estates and was reputed to be a wealthy man in his own right. Although Boni, in his memoirs, has described his cousin as something of a monster of duplicity, the Duc, who was ten years older than Anna, had put his youthful indiscretions behind him, and in any event was of a different stripe than Boni, the exquisite wastrel. The Duc and Duchesse lived lives of quiet elegance and grandeur. The petulantly romantic little girl of Lyndhurst became a great lady doomed to a life of great sorrows. Her three sons by Boni died young. Her only son by the Duc killed himself because his parents refused to sanction his marriage to an older woman. When the Duc died in 1937, Anna was left a lonely, aging widow in a foreign land. Her daughter by the Duc, Violette, Comtesse de Pourtales, and her grandchildren were thoroughly French. Their only connection to the Goulds was that, when grandmama died, they would inherit the principal of the trust for her benefit under the will of a strange and legendary *américain* named Jay Gould, who had died many years before they were born. It was indeed a substantial connection, but hardly a consoling one for the Duchesse.

Although her life was rooted by tragedy in France, and Lyndhurst was superfluous from any rational point of view, the Duchesse was still a Gould and could, if she wished, afford sentimental gestures on a grand scale. In 1939, when the market was flooded with great houses that could hardly be given away, it is conceivable that the former Anna Gould was the only person alive who had both the means and the desire to prevent Lyndhurst from remaining empty and unwanted until put to some ignoble utilitarian use, or from being demolished to make way for a housing development. For the Duchesse, Lyndhurst was far more than an old house where she had lived; it was the place where she could recapture the nostalgic glow of cherished childhood memories. Half a century later, even the prissy tyranny of Helen's guardianship could seem quaint and endearing. And the bitter memories of her marriage with poor silly Boni could be forgotten in the place where they had spent a romantic honeymoon so many long winters ago.

As impervious to reason as when she had been a schoolgirl who would have married a handsome young actor if George and Helen had not forcefully intervened, the Duchesse came flying to the rescue of Lyndhurst by buying it from her sister's estate. The price she paid—$277,635—was, perhaps, more than fair. Yet practical wisdom to the contrary, the Duchesse's sentimental gesture was to prove a sound investment, financially as well

as emotionally. And Lyndhurst, at last, had as mistress a real *duchesse* to match its architectural glories.

Each year, accompanied by her beloved Pekingese, the Duchesse came back to spend six months in the nostalgic surroundings of her childhood. Faithfully installing herself in the small tower bedroom with the oriel window which had been hers as a little girl, she grew older and lonelier and more sentimental. Her brother Frank died in 1956, and Howard in 1959. The little dogs

In 1884 George Jay Gould married Edith Kingdon, famous on Broadway for her hourglass figure. The sands of time were running a bit thick when she posed with her pearls in the nineties.

died, too, one by one, and were lovingly buried in elaborate leaden caskets. But Anna lived on, the last of the Goulds who had grown up at Lyndhurst. In the summer of 1961, with her health failing badly, she returned to France to be with her daughter and grandchildren. When she said farewell to Lyndhurst, it was a sad parting, for she knew she would never return, and its fate weighed heavily upon her. Two years before, when she had made her last will and testament, she had left Lyndhurst to the National Trust for Historic Preservation, to be permanently maintained "as a non-profit museum in memory of my mother, Helen D. Gould, and my father, Jay Gould." She had also left a substantial endowment fund to provide for its maintenance. But since then the opposition both of her heirs and of Tarrytown itself to such a bequest had confused and upset her.

Among the citizens of Irvington and Tarrytown, who referred unkindly to the Duchesse as a "mystery woman"

By 1908, when this picture was taken, the romance between Edith and George had become mostly a matter of posture, and he was within a few years of crossing the bar sinister with a young mistress.

because she wished to shut out the present and live in the past and could, when necessary, be quite disagreeable about it, the ultimate fate of Lyndhurst had long been the subject of speculation. The Duchesse was the largest residential taxpayer in the community, and her 550 acres were surpassed in size only by the 3,500 acres of the Rockefellers' sequestered demesne at Pocantico Hills. Citizens shuddered at the thought of acreage so desirable for commercial and residential exploitation being permanently removed from the tax rolls.

"Green property," as such tax-exempt oases of undeveloped real estate are sometimes covetously known, is all very well, but frequently, as the Tarrytown *Daily News* pointed out, the "green that counts most is in Uncle Sam's currency." When word of the Duchesse's death finally came, late in November, 1961, the *News* wasted little time on the customary amenities. A banner headline across the front page proclaimed, "MYSTERY WOMAN'S WILL CASTS TAX SHADOW," and the obituary itself was concerned less with the fabled life of the deceased than with the fact that Lyndhurst had been bequeathed to a tax-exempt institution. The *News*, however, did offer its readers a ray of hope—and a gentle pat on its own back. The Duchesse, for all of her aloofness, was known to have been an ardent follower of the paper and, due to its "convincing editorials," was reliably reported to have said that she did not wish to do anything that might "hurt" the community. Thus, the *News* was banking heavily on a later will from which any well-intentioned but misguided bequest of Lyndhurst away from the family would be eliminated.

The great expectations of the *Daily News* were, alas, to be only partially fulfilled. The Duchesse had never quite gotten around to making a new will. During the last year of her life she had suffered severely from an affliction—prevalent especially among rich, infirm, and elderly females—that thrives in an environment of idle, self-seeking children, poor relations, lawyers, doctors, nurses, and overly solicitous gossips. Although it is a disease to which no name has ever been given, its symptoms are none the less acute: excessive vanity, pique, sentimentality, and indecision appear in a chronic rash of codicils.

Between January 25, 1961, and November 23, 1961, the Duchesse added five codicils to her original will of September 10, 1959. In the final codicil, made five days before her death, she revoked her original bequest of Lyndhurst to the National Trust and left it to be divided among her Talleyrand daughter and her four Castellane granddaughters. While deathbed codicils are not cloaked in the same legal majesty as the will itself, the shadow cast by Lyndhurst over Tarrytown was now perceptibly diminished. Dubious though the validity of the fateful codicil might prove to be as a binding legal instrument, the National Trust was a government agency accountable to Congress for its acts and would, it was felt, hardly presume to contest its disinheritance without the support of the community.

The National Trust for Historic Preservation in the United States is a charitable, educational, and nonprofit corporation, created in 1949 by an act of Congress ". . . to facilitate public participation in the preservation of sites, buildings and objects of national significance or interest and providing a national trust for historic preservation." In the realm of federal bureaucracy the National Trust is a pygmy, unsupported by public funds except for minor administrative expenses. It is dependent almost entirely on legacies, gifts, donations, and membership fees, and while its operations are sometimes hampered by lack of funds and its acts are theoretically subject to congressional scrutiny, in practice it is a relatively independent government agency staffed by professionals dedicated to the cause of historic preservation. By 1961 it had acquired seven properties of historical and cultural significance to preserve and administer for public benefit. Lyndhurst, considered solely as the most illustrious surviving example of nineteenth-century neo-Gothic residential architecture in America, would be a notable accession to its domain. As a museum piece illuminating the now-vanished way of life of an era, Lyndhurst was a preservationst's dream. The National Trust did not intend to give it up without a fight.

In spite of Lyndhurst's obvious cultural and historical significance, the village trustees of Tarrytown were amazed and angered to learn that the National Trust was reluctant to accept its disinheritance gracefully and had refused to agree to the probate of the will if the final codicil revoking its legacy was included. There seemed no reason for alarm, however, as it was also revealed that the heirs of the Duchesse were firmly opposed to giving anything away to *les américains*. Lyndhurst, valued at $1,269,592 by the state tax appraiser, and with its acreage potentially worth considerably more in a rising real-estate market, comprised a substantial part of the Duchesse's net estate of $5,500,000 before taxes. Aside from crass monetary considerations, French aristocrats are traditionally opposed to parting with family property under any circumstances. Even one in such dire straits as the late Boni de Castellane could boast, in his disdainful memoir, *How I Discovered America*, that "there is no sacrifice too great for us to make in order to retain these homes in our hands, because they form part of the family, and represent tombs of past and future generations." The prospects of the National Trust seemed hardly bright, and indignation in Tarrytown subsided as counsel for the contending factions settled down to fight it out behind closed doors.

The atmosphere of family intrigue surrounding the Duchesse in the ancient castle at Marais where she had lived out the few remaining months of her life, a prisoner of her age and illness, had been far from favorable to her original bequest of Lyndhurst to the National Trust. That the de Castellane and Talleyrand branches of her family had been vying for her favor is evident from the first and second codicils. There are signs in the first codicil that her granddaughter Diane de Castellane's position as favorite was being undermined. In the second codicil Diane's downfall was made official: the

Château du Marais, a former domain of the de Castellanes, was taken from her and given to the Duchesse's daughter, Violette, Comtesse de Pourtales. The triumph of the Talleyrands was poignantly revealed in one seemingly trivial bequest: "I give all dogs which I may own at the time of my death to my granddaughter, Anna de Pourtales."

Both factions, however, were firmly united in opposition to the National Trust, for there was far more at stake than Lyndhurst. There was also the tenth article of the original will, which would establish a trust fund valued at approximately three million dollars to provide for the maintenance of Lyndhurst, and which would reduce the value of the residuary estate to be distributed among the heirs to a mere $421,000. Certainly the Duchesse, who had been accustomed to an annual income in excess of so paltry a sum, did not intend to leave her own flesh and blood in want; but she felt—at least while she had been safe in her tower at Lyndhurst, secure from outside influences—that her daughter and granddaughters would be more than amply provided for as the remaindermen and sole inheritors of the twelve-million-dollar trust of which she was the life beneficiary under the will of her father. Unfortunately for Lyndhurst, not even the Comtesse de Pourtales, who would receive one third of the trust fund, was amiably disposed to this view. The three daughters of the Duchesse's deceased son, Boni de Castellane II, who would receive but one ninth each, were, presumably, proportionately less contented.

By the end of September the harried old lady that the Duchesse had become was ready to add a third codicil to her will. She was so ill that she was unable to sign it, but it was duly attested and notarized with the punctilious flourish with which the French invest such matters, and was later offered for probate by her executors. For Lyndhurst the vital clause read, "I direct that all my property situated in the United States, at Lyndhurst . . . is to go to the three branches of my heirs. . . . Accordingly, I formally revoke the previous legacy that I made on the subject of that property."

Somehow, during the next two weeks, the defiant stubbornness with which as a schoolgirl she had once plagued her sister, Helen, came to life again, and on October 12 she made a fourth codicil. The actual provisions of this codicil are not known, since it was later revoked and French law forbids the disclosure of nullified legal instruments. Under the circumstances, however, it is plausible to assume that one of the purposes of this vanished codicil was to rescue Lyndhurst from the hungry maws of real-estate operators.

When the Duchesse signed the fifth and final codicil on November 23, five days before her death, in the sitting room of her private suite in the Château du Marais, she was in a wheel chair. But she was fully and rather regally dressed in a red cape with gold fringe. It is true that she spoke in French as little as possible, but that had always been her custom. It is also true that her hand shook so badly that it was necessary for a nurse to hold her wrist as she made her signature. Although her daughter, the Comtesse de Pourtales, whose favored position in regard to the Duchesse's French property was reaffirmed by the final codicil, was known to have been in the castle at the time, she was not actually in the room at the moment when the codicil was signed. The Duchesse's signature, though but a faint, barely legible scrawl, was incontestably hers. Later, not even agents of the F.B.I., with the full majesty of the United States government behind them, could shake the conviction of the witnesses that her mind was alert and clear and that she knew exactly what she was doing. The fact that she misstated the year of her birth, giving it as 1878 instead of 1875, could be attributed, even by the F.B.I., to a poignant remnant of feminine vanity.

While the final codicil renewed the revocation of the bequest of Lyndhurst to the National Trust that had been made in the third codicil, it was phrased in such a way as to indicate that the Duchesse had not really made up her mind what to do, and that she still may have been clinging to some hope that her original intentions might be realized.

At the outset of legal hostilities between the heirs and the National Trust, the destiny of Lyndhurst seemed to rest entirely upon the validity of that final codicil. The climate in which it had been executed was ideal to support at least a suspicion that it was invalid due to testa-

mentary incapacity and to undue influence. But the codicil itself had been meticulously and flawlessly executed by the French notary, and convincing proof of such shadowy charges is always an extremely difficult matter.

The effort of the National Trust to reclaim its bequest and preserve Lyndhurst for the nation was strongly supported by the cultural elite, then so prominent in the Kennedy administration. Its unique role in affairs of state was demonstrated by the entry into the dispute, as a party to the action, of the United States of America. This unexpected and rather curious move was justified by the Attorney General's office on the grounds that under the terms of the National Trust's charter the United States of America had a contingent interest in all properties held by the National Trust. The appearance of the Attorney General of the United States in the case brought forth the minions of the Federal Bureau of Investigation, and in the early summer of 1962 F.B.I. agents were dispatched abroad to interrogate witnesses to the codicil and, if possible, to develop evidence of the misty existence of undue influence.

The heirs, highly incensed by what they considered a brutal and unwarranted intrusion by the U.S.A. into their private affairs, denounced it as an act of aggression by a foreign power. Lengthy fusillades of motions and cross-motions were exchanged during the latter half of 1962 and on into 1963. Counsel for the heirs argued heatedly that any alleged contingent interest the U.S.A. might have was far too remote and speculative to be relevant to the present proceeding, and the tactics of the F.B.I. stirred them to flights of indignant legal eloquence.

The victory in this fierce preliminary skirmish went to

TEXT CONTINUED ON PAGE 64

Some of Jay Gould's progeny married very well: the handsome Marjorie, for instance, George's eldest daughter, became Mrs. Anthony Drexel, Jr., in 1910. Others had less luck and more trouble: at right, Howard's second wife, a German actress named Margaret Mosheim, in divorce court in 1947, when Howard was 76.

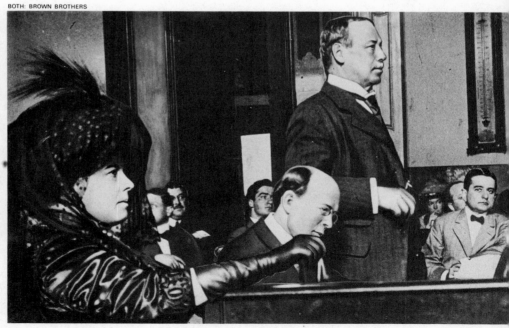

61

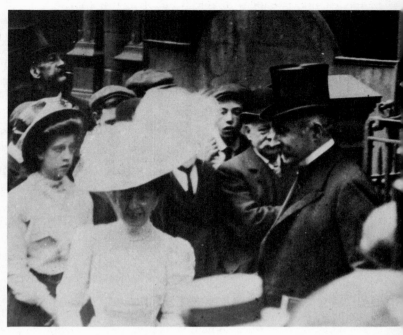

Two of Jay Gould's grandchildren, offspring of George and Edith Gould, were Jay III (above), a lifelong court-tennis champion, and Vivien (below), who in 1911 married a dashing Britisher, the fifth Baron Decies. The Gould family liked his title and the Baron liked their money, but apparently the marriage was happy.

Jay Gould's daughter Anna had mixed luck with titled husbands. In 1895 she married the penniless Count Boni de Castellane (above) in a fashionable ceremony (below) at brother George's New York town house. They were later divorced. Her marriage (left) in 1908 to the wealthy Duc de Talleyrand-Périgord was much happier.

the heirs. On February 14, 1963, Surrogate Joseph A. Cox ruled that the United States was not a proper party to the proceeding, and the National Trust was left to fight it out alone. With the United States and the F.B.I. removed from the field, the heirs forged ahead. The will and the first and second codicils were at last admitted to probate, but a counteroffensive by the National Trust resulted in the denial, on March 19, 1963, of probate to the third codicil, in which the Duchesse had first revoked the original bequest of Lyndhurst, but which she herself had not signed. This brought matters to a stalemate,

Each of Jay Gould's daughters saved Lyndhurst by paying over a quarter of a million dollars for it when it was put on the market—Helen in 1905, and Anna in 1939. Here the two filial proprietors appear with typically contrasting costumes and miens.

with the outcome apparently resting on the fate of the final codicil. A long and costly litigation, with the odds in favor of the heirs, now seemed inevitable.

This unhappy situation continued for more than a year until finally, after long and secret negotiations, the legal wizards on both sides conjured up a magic formula that would allow everyone, including themselves, to retire from the field with acceptable shares of the booty. In a compromise agreement dated May 1, 1964, the contending parties agreed that "after due consideration of all of the facts and circumstances" it would

be "in their best interest to compromise and adjust any issues which might be raised by the filing of objections to the Codicil [the fifth] dated November 23, 1961, and thereby avoid the delay and expense of extensive litigation." Although the National Trust never actually retreated from its position that the final codicil was invalid, the withdrawal of its objections was the key to the solution of the problem. With the codicil admitted to probate and the original bequest of Lyndhurst revoked, the consciences of the heirs and the legal position of the executors were technically sanctified. In return, the executors ceded Lyndhurst and the greater part of its acreage to the National Trust, which, in turn, relinquished its claim to the three-million-dollar endowment fund that had been perhaps the real sticking point with the heirs all along.

But the indispensable ingredient in the magic formula was the almost unprecedented generosity of the Commissioner of Internal Revenue, who was somehow prevailed upon to accept a whopping reduction in the amount of the federal estate tax to which he was lawfully entitled. The compromise agreement did not become effective until the commissioner agreed in writing that the full value of Lyndhurst "shall be deductible . . . from decedent's gross estate in computing the amount of Federal Estate Tax to be imposed upon decedent's estate." Also to be allowed as a deduction were fees and reasonable disbursements, totalling $243,525.16, to be paid to the legal experts who had concocted the agreement. It was indeed a neat arrangement.

For the better part of the two and a half years consumed in legal strife and negotiation, Tarrytown had been left simmering in ignorance, and the village trustees were smouldering with resentment at the discourtesy of the National Trust in failing to keep them informed on a matter of vital local concern. When at last, on August 19, 1964, a brief communiqué revealed that an agreement granting Lyndhurst to the National Trust had already been reached, the trustees were stunned. Details were scarce, but it was definitely known that Congress had already approved the compromise agreement in a rider hastily tacked onto a minor revenue bill and that President Johnson soon would sign it into law.

The Tarrytown *Daily News*, its "convincing editorials" gone for naught, referred scathingly to the rider as a "slider," and painted a grim picture of the future. Hordes of unruly sightseers would descend upon the town, creating parking problems and traffic congestion and bringing in their wake a garish Coney Island mélange of reeking hot-dog stands and fly-by-night souvenir shoppes.

A few days later word leaked out that the decisive factor in persuading the heirs to part with one of their ancestral homes had been the generosity of the Commissioner of Internal Revenue in allowing the estate to claim Lyndhurst as a deduction and thus reduce the federal estate tax by approximately $830,000. The *Daily News* indignantly branded this a "giveaway" of public funds and grudgingly praised Senator Wayne Morse, usually regarded as a troublemaking maverick, for his honesty in being the sole legislator to question it.

Tarrytown was not yet ready to concede defeat. Amid the confusion of garbled press releases, George B. Case, a village trustee and chairman of the village planning board, wrote both to the National Trust and to one of the executors for more specific information as to the terms of the compromise agreement. When a satisfactory reply from neither of them was forthcoming, Jay Gould himself, and his unsavory reputation, were rudely resurrected. The village board, now bristling with righteous indignation, unanimously adopted a resolution petitioning Congress "to see that justice is done and honor restored by revoking the legislation . . . authorizing the museum." And once again, more than seventy years after his death, that strange man who had seemed to love orchids more than people and who had craved some mystic infinity of wealth and power more than his own life was to prove a convenient scapegoat.

"Whereas," this curious document reads in part, "the name of Jay Gould is one to be remembered but certainly not for honor and exaltation. . . .

"Whereas, decent law abiding citizens would welcome any fitting memorial to a worthy American, they question any memorial to a person with the reputation of Jay Gould."

Perhaps the petition would have been more impressive if it had candidly presented the burdens of "green property" for communities already saddled with fiscal problems that Mr. Gould himself could not have evaded. Even the *Daily News* wondered why it was necessary to bring back Jay Gould. Large sums of his supposedly tainted money had been gratefully accepted by the community from his daughter Helen, who had been a notorious soft touch and Tarrytown's Number One philanthropist.

Mr. Case, though one of a dwindling minority in Tarrytown who remembers and appreciates Miss Gould and her good works, has never retreated by so much as a single "whereas" from the petition of which he was the most vigorous and sincere exponent. The petition itself, presented in the midst of a presidential election campaign, was doomed to be a futile gesture. Congress was in no mood to spend time on soothing the wounded pride and pocketbook of a small community in one of the nation's wealthiest counties.

On October 30 Surrogate Cox formally approved the compromise agreement between the National Trust and the heirs of the Duchesse. Lyndhurst and some 450 of its original domain of 550 acres were now incontestably the property of the National Trust for Historic Preservation, the duly authorized custodian of the true owner, the people of the United States. The remaining acres went to the heirs as a consolation for giving up one of their ancestral homes. Even Tarrytown was somewhat mollified when it was announced that nearly four hundred acres would be sold by the National Trust, with the proceeds to be used to set up a permanent endowment fund for the benefit of Lyndhurst. When it was sold, in September of the following year, for subdivision as a residential development, it netted less than expected: only $1,250,000. Mr. Case and his fellow trustees could hardly be expected to refrain from pointing out that in their petition they had warned of just such an outcome.

It is true that the income from a conservatively managed $1,250,000 trust fund may be inadequate to support Lyndhurst in the style to which it became accustomed during the long reign of the Goulds. But the pride of the National Trust in its properties and the diligence and ingenuity of its staff should not be discounted. In any event, Lyndhurst is at last as secure as it is possible to be from the normal legal and financial perils that beset mortal man.

Lyndhurst was opened to the public in June, 1965, and was officially dedicated on May 20, 1966. Governor Nelson Rockefeller was the principal speaker at the dedication ceremonies, and his presence drew a line of well-mannered pickets outside the entrance gates protesting not against Lyndhurst but against the proposed Hudson River Expressway. "Millions For Roads," read some of the bitter placards, "Not One Cent For Beauty!" Among the pickets was Jay Gould's nemesis, George B. Case, still tilting at the windmills of "big" government's encroaching on the rights of local communities to govern themselves. This time he was on Lyndhurst's side. The expressway, as originally planned, would have violated Lyndhurst's territorial rights along the riverfront where the yacht landing used to be.

The star of this auspicious occasion in the life of what Mr. Hone had too hastily predicted would one day be known as "Paulding's Folly" was Diane de Castellane, Duchesse de Mouchy. Madame de Mouchy, one of the granddaughters of Anna Gould and Boni de Castellane, was filled with pride and enthusiasm. Now that the legal strife was over, she had become an ardent supporter of the preservation of Lyndhurst. Her grandmother would have been overjoyed. This happy ending to what had once appeared to be an inevitably sad story was undoubtedly a truer expression of the real wishes of the former Anna Gould than the codicil made under such dire circumstance. Long live Lyndhurst!

Frank Kintrea is a free-lance writer from upstate New York whose special interest is business history.

Few Americans remember even hazily what they were doing on the night of June 13, 1942. John C. Cullen remembers exactly what he was doing. He remembers with special vividness his activities at around twenty-five minutes past midnight. At that moment of time he was patrolling the lonely Atlantic beach near Amagansett, Long Island, 105 miles east of New York City. He did this every night—a six-mile hike. At that moment he was coming out of a thick patch of fog to run head-on into what seemed to be a Grade B movie thriller, but which turned out to be real life, with intimations of real death.

Cullen was twenty-one, a rookie coastguardsman, unarmed. America, at war with the Axis powers more than three thousand miles away, was yet worried enough about invasion, sabotage, and sneak attacks that houses were blacked out and coastlines were watched. Many good citizens thought this an excess of caution. Cullen himself says now that the last thing he expected to encounter was a party of invading Nazis just landed from a German submarine.

(Today, at forty-seven a substantial family man who represents a large Long Island dairy co-operative, he retains a sense of having participated in a chunk of history so implausible that one would doubt it were it not all down in the records. "I suppose I've rehashed the story a thousand times," he says. "I had no weapon more dangerous than a flashlight and a Coast Guard flare gun, and I still feel lucky I got out of it alive.")

A man emerged from the mist—not too surprising, for some fishermen stayed out all hours in the summer. Cullen shone his torch on the stranger's face. "Who are you?" he asked.

The man—middle-sized, neither young nor old, gaunt, and with cavernous eyes—smiled. "We're fishermen from Southampton and ran aground here," he said. He identified himself as George Davis. Three of his companions were visible only as dark blobs in the mist. One of them came closer and shouted something in a foreign language that Cullen thought was German, and which angered Davis. "Shut up, you damn fool," he growled. "Everything is all right. Go back to the boys and stay with them."

("That jarred me, made me suspicious," Cullen recalls. "And I could see that this fellow was very nervous. Why should he be so nervous if he was O.K.?")

From then on events took a turn melodramatic enough to make a young coastguardsman believe himself gripped by fantasy. He suggested that Davis accompany him to the Amagansett Coast Guard station less than a quarter of a mile away. Davis refused. "Now wait a minute," Davis said. "You don't know what this is all about." He became quietly menacing, asking Cullen if he had a father and mother who would mourn him and saying, "I don't want to kill you." He reached into his pocket, but instead of a pistol he produced a wallet and offered Cullen $150, which he quickly raised to $300, to forget what he had seen. Cullen took the money to be agreeable, knowing he had no chance against four men, and also because it occurred to him that no one would believe his story unless he had evidence to prove it. For all he knew, guns might be covering him in the darkness. Cullen heard Davis murmur, "Forget about this," and then he headed back toward his station. ("I made it in record time," he recalls.)

Boatswain's Mate Carl R. Jenette, acting officer in charge, listened to this story with understandable incredulity. He counted the money and found that Cullen had been shortchanged—two fifties, five twenties, and six tens, totalling $260. He telephoned the station's commander, Warrant Officer Warren Barnes. While

Wartime America's nerves were jumpy. One foggy night on a deserted Long Island beach a young coastguardsman heard the muffled engines of a submarine offshore, and suddenly eight shadowy figures loomed up out of the mist

THE SPIES WHO CAME IN FROM THE SEA

By W. A. SWANBERG

F.B.I. - N.Y.C.
65-11065- N4506
JUNE 24 1942

Georg Johann Dasch

Barnes hurriedly dressed, Jenette armed Cullen and three other "beach pounders" and raced with them over the dunes to the scene of the improbability.

Davis and his companions were gone. The coast-guardsmen could smell fuel oil and could hear a throbbing engine; offshore they could see the superstructure of a submarine splashed by wavelets. It was the *U-202* under Lieutenant Commander Lindner, which had run lightly aground and was freeing herself, moving eastward. ("She had a blinker light," Cullen remembers. "We ducked behind a dune, not wanting to get shelled, until she slid away.")

A search of the beach in the morning disclosed: an empty pack of German cigarettes; four heavy, waterproof oaken boxes buried in the sand; a gray duffel bag, also buried, containing four soggy German marine uniforms. The boxes contained brick-sized blocks of high explosives, bombs disguised as lumps of coal, bomb-timing mechanisms of German make, and innocent-looking "pen-and-pencil sets" that were actually incendiary weapons.

By this time the affair looked decidedly sinister. The Federal Bureau of Investigation took charge, trying to pick up the trail of "George Davis" and his men, hoping to prevent a repetition of the disastrously efficient German sabotage of World War I that had demolished the Kingsland arsenal and the Black Tom munitions plant in New Jersey. Ira Baker, the Long Island Railroad's Amagansett station agent, remembered four men, one of them answering Davis' description, buying tickets for the first morning train to New York City. Now the four men were swallowed up by the metropolis.

Behind this menacing business lay a curious Nazi seminary of sabotage at Quentz Lake, forty miles west of Berlin near Brandenburg. Established by the *Abwehr*, the German military intelligence headed by Admiral Wilhelm Canaris and Colonel Erwin von Lahousen, the school had received a direct order from Hitler to train specialists for the destruction of vital factories and communications in America. It was a crash program representing German fear of American industrial might. Perhaps this was why its high requirements for secret agents—men who not only qualified in intelligence and courage but who also spoke English and were familiar with the United States—were sometimes allowed to slide. Indeed, George Davis, whose real name was Georg Johann Dasch, was hardly the kind of operative one might meet in the pages of John Le Carré.

Born in Speyer-am-Rhein in 1903, Dasch landed in Philadelphia as a stowaway in 1922. Familiar with German and French, he soon learned English, but he became disgruntled because he could find work only as a waiter. He followed this calling at hotels and restaurants in New York, Miami, Los Angeles, and San Francisco. After his marriage in 1930 to Rose Marie Guille, a Pennsylvania-born hairdresser, he visited Germany with his bride. When they returned to America, Dasch again was seen at some fairly good restaurants, but only as a man with a tray.

Meanwhile the propaganda coming out of the Fatherland confirmed his belief that he was meant for better things. The beginning of the European war in 1939 made up his mind. He haunted the German consulate in New York, begging them to get him back into Germany. His passage was arranged in March of 1941, and in Berlin, Dasch met thirty-six-year-old Lieutenant Walter Kappe, a Nazi intelligence officer who from 1925 to 1937 had worked as a newspaperman in Chicago and Cincinnati and had wound up in New York as press chief for the Hitler-loving German-American Bund. Dasch's English was good, so Kappe landed him a job monitoring

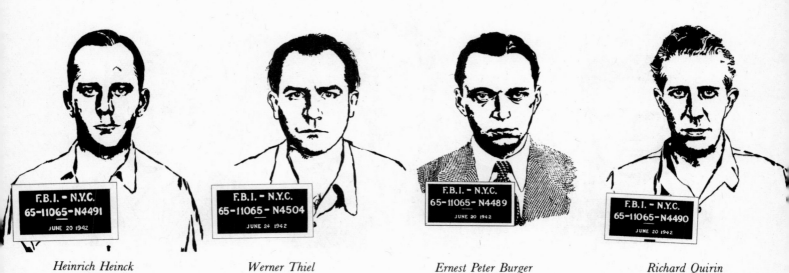

Heinrich Heinck   *Werner Thiel*   *Ernest Peter Burger*   *Richard Quirin*

American broadcasts. In February, 1942, when Kappe was selected to superintend the "American branch" of the Quentz Lake school for saboteurs, he picked Dasch as his first pupil. Among the others in the student body were seven who figure in this account, all of whom had spent years in America:

Violin-playing Ernest Peter Burger, from Augsburg, was only seventeen when he joined Hitler's gang in the abortive Munich beer-hall putsch of 1923. Immigrating to America in 1927, he worked as a machinist in Milwaukee and in Detroit, joined the Michigan National Guard and also the German-American Bund, and in 1933 became a citizen; but he returned to Germany that same year when Hitler became chancellor. He rose swiftly to become aide to Captain Ernst Röhm, head of the storm troopers—a connection that became a liability when Röhm was liquidated in the 1934 blood purge. Thereafter Burger had the inevitable troubles with the Gestapo. In 1940 he was imprisoned for seventeen months, occasionally tortured, and his pregnant wife was grilled so mercilessly that she had a miscarriage. After his release, however, his standing was partially restored, and he became a student at Quentz Lake.

Edward Kerling, born in Wiesbaden in 1909, had joined the Nazi party in 1928 and yet had gone to America the following year. He worked in a Brooklyn packing plant, then became a chauffeur, handling the wheel for Ely Culbertson, the bridge expert, and other wealthy people. He married, but soon separated from his wife. A loyal Bundist, he also kept up his dues-paid membership in the Brown Shirts, so that when he returned to Germany in July, 1940, he had considerable seniority.

Richard Quirin, a Berliner, was nineteen when he came to the United States in 1927. He worked as a mechanic in Syracuse, Schenectady, and New York City and joined the Bund. His return to the Fatherland in 1939 came about because he was out of work at the time, Germany had started a policy of paying the return fare for the faithful, and the news about *Der Führer* excited his feelings of nationalism.

Heinrich Heinck, born in Hamburg in 1907, had entered the United States illegally in 1926. After working in New York City as a handyman, then as a machinist, he was swept away by the stirring rites of the Bund, and in 1939 he also leaped at the "free return trip" offer.

Hermann Otto Neubauer, born in Hamburg in 1910, had been a cook and hotel worker in Hartford and Chicago from 1931 until 1940, when his Bund-inspired Nazi loyalty drew him back home.

Werner Thiel, born in Dortmund in 1907, came to America at twenty to work as a toolmaker and in other jobs in Philadelphia, Detroit, and Los Angeles. He followed the pattern in his wholehearted embracing of the Bund (Dasch was the only nonmember) and in accepting a German-paid return trip after the war began in 1939.

Herbert Hans Haupt was brought to America by his parents from Stettin as a five-year-old, grew up in Chicago, and became an optical worker there. He had little recollection of Germany, but his father, although naturalized, was such a loyal Nazi that he might as well have been in Prussia. Young Haupt drilled with the Bund in an Illinois cornfield. Still, his return to Germany was motivated by prudence as well as national feeling. Discovering that his Chicago girl friend was pregnant, he fled to Mexico in June of 1941. The German consul in Mexico City, regarding him as useful timber, gave him money and arranged his passage to Germany by way of Japan. Haupt, born in 1919, was the youngest member of the student body and a lady-killer.

During April and part of May, 1942, these eight men were hurry-up classmates at Quentz Farm, where their teachers were experts—two of them doctors of philoso-

Edward Kerling

Hermann Otto Neubauer

Herbert Hans Haupt

phy—in explosives, chemistry, electricity, and allied arts useful in destruction. In the surrounding fields small bridges and lengths of railroad track had been built, and here the students could lay practice demolition charges under the supervision of their instructors. They were expected to study the American newspapers and magazines passed around among them and to be posted on current American news, slang, and song hits. Finally they were taken to factories in Berlin, Bitterfeld, and Aachen and shown how the destruction of one vital production process could knock out a whole plant. They were saluted with a "graduation" dinner complete with wines, and their mission was designated Operation Pastorius, after Franz Pastorius, the first German immigrant to America, who landed in 1683.

Each man (except for the two American citizens, Burger and Haupt, who could safely use their own names) was given a fictitious identity and forged papers to support it—passport, draft card, ration coupons, and driver's license. Each of the fraudulent six memorized a fake past history.

On May 22, 1942, Lieutenant Kappe and the eight took the express train to Nazi-occupied Paris, where they had a two-day binge—theatres, night clubs, women—courtesy of the Third Reich. Thence they travelled to the submarine base at Lorient, the take-off point. Dasch, the leader of one four-man team, had with him Burger, Quirin, and Heinck. Kerling, the other leader, had under him Neubauer, Thiel, and Haupt. To each team Kappe gave about ninety thousand dollars in United States currency, the leader carrying the bulk of it—a sum intended to cover possible bribes as well as expenses. Each team leader was also given an ordinary white handkerchief on which was written, in invisible ink that could be brought out by ammonia fumes, the names and addresses of a Lisbon mail drop that would reach the *Abwehr*, and two dependable sources of help in the United States. On the night of May 26 Kerling and his men boarded the *U-584*, under Lieutenant Commander Deeke, and soon were plowing westward in the Atlantic, bound for Florida. Two nights later Dasch and his group were off in the *U-202* for Long Island.

The landing of the saboteurs near Amagansett was made in an inflated rubber boat with the aid of sailors from the *U-202*. The four were clad in German marine fatigue uniforms on the theory that if captured at once they would be treated as prisoners of war (that is, interned) rather than being shot as spies. They quickly changed into mufti, buried their cache, and after the brush with coastguardsman Cullen, went on to New York, where Dasch and Burger took rooms at the Governor Clinton Hotel across from Pennsylvania Station. Heinck and Quirin registered at the Hotel Martinique.

Now the men and their mission took on a complexion of *opéra bouffe*. They lacked the close acquaintance and implicit trust that was essential for the success of an assignment of such high risk and long duration. The morale of three of them had sagged during the sixteen-day submarine voyage—a Spartan journey made fearful when the U-boat had to hit bottom to escape American destroyers and was shaken, though not damaged, by depth charges. They actually disliked each other. Burger, the solid one of the group, had ice in his veins and was equal to any risk; but he was not forgetting what the Gestapo had done to him, and besides, he had lost all faith in Dasch. Quirin tended to be moody and quarrelsome. Heinck had already exhibited a weakness for liquor and loose talk that was potentially fatal. Dasch himself was undergoing the cold shivers. Their narrow escape from the Coast Guard had been a vivid reminder of the dangers they faced. The psychological pressures peculiar to those most isolated of all creatures, secret agents, were oppressive.

They had too much time to think, for their orders were to spend about ninety days in preparation before launching any sabotage. They were loaded with more money than any of them had ever seen before; and they spent it on snappy American summer clothes and on food that seemed Lucullan after the leaner German war rations. Dasch, the knowing ex-waiter, escorted his crew to restaurants he liked—the Swiss Chalet, the Kungsholm, Dinty Moore's, and an Automat near Macy's.

On Sunday morning, only some thirty hours after they had landed, Dasch and Burger had a long talk at their hotel during which Dasch dropped subtle hints of his own doubts in order to determine whether his sidekick felt the same way and could be trusted. It must have been instantly apparent to Burger that with the leader in such a frame of mind the mission would surely fail, and he had better get clear. Reassured at last, Dasch said he intended to betray the whole plot (and his accomplices) to the F.B.I. According to the two men's later testimony, they agreed to this at once. Dasch felt that by exposing the plot he would become an American hero celebrated in headlines and honored by the President.

At 7:51 on Sunday evening, with Burger standing near the telephone booth, Dasch called the New York F.B.I. office and talked with Agent Dean F. McWhorter. Identifying himself as Frank Daniel Pastorius, he said he was recently from Germany. "I want you to know," he said, "that I shall get in touch with your Washington office next Thursday or Friday. I have some important information." When McWhorter asked what the information was, the caller said it was of such moment that only J. Edgar Hoover himself could have it, and then hung up. McWhorter, accustomed to crank calls, nevertheless made a record of the conversation.

CONTINUED ON PAGE 87

THE GHOST OF SAGAMORE HILL

There used to be a chain in front of the driveway at Sagamore Hill. My grandmother put it there to stop the hordes of curiosity seekers who came to Sagamore, thinking perhaps that no one lived there anymore. So, grumbling, my father would stop the car to let us in, and I could, for a moment, observe from a distance the old gray house brooding in its nest of stately elms.

I felt, with that peculiar instinct of a child, that this large Victorian structure had some kind of life of its own. And as we drove under the porte-cochère my sense of adventure quickened, for I always anticipated these visits with an excitement the late master of the house would have appreciated. I was lucky as a small boy to spend many weeks of my summer and winter vacations at Sagamore Hill, and adventure was always there.

We were a large family he left behind. Besides my immediate family—my parents and three sisters—there were my boisterous uncles Ted and Kermit, with their wives, the brilliant and elegant Auntie Eleanor and the glamorous Auntie Belle; my fairy godmother, Auntie Ethel (Derby), and her kindly doctor-husband Uncle Dick; and the mysterious and romantic figure of "Auntie Sister" (Alice Roosevelt Longworth), who lived far away in Washington and made a brief, queenly appearance from time to time. (We never quite understood as children how an aunt could be "Sister" as well, but eventually found out that she had always been called Sister by our parents' generation. Her real name, Alice, was never used in the family.) And with all these came masses of cousins—a dozen or so—quite a few close to my age.

Grandmother was an awesome chatelaine. She ruled the house and its unruly visitors in her soft and precise voice, an iron hand scarcely hidden in the velvet glove. Only when we were older did we realize she was small and frail. To us she seemed eight feet tall, and although she never raised that quiet voice, it could take on an icy tone that made even the largest and strongest tremble.

Even so, she was not the absolute ruler of Sagamore Hill. My grandfather was—even though he had died many years before, when I was less than a year old. The house had been left exactly as it was the day he died, and his spirit permeated every corner of it, as well as the grounds outside. Now I realize the house was truly haunted, but we children would never have called it that, because our ghost was a kindly one who kept a jolly and benevolent eye on all of us, balancing Grandmother's essential severity as he had in life. He was a beloved and familiar figure—our hero and our playmate. All the activities of the house followed the patterns he had set during his lifetime—the food, the games, the celebrations, the stories, and even the phrases and words he had made so much his own. He just had too much vitality to die and leave all those grandchildren deprived of his companionship.

I felt his presence strongly the minute I came through the door into a hall cluttered with his possessions—an elephant's foot stuffed with his canes, the walls festooned with majestic heads of African beasts. His study was on the right, and I always liked to sit at his desk a minute and look out the large window at the elms. I was half

A memoir by
ARCHIBALD B. ROOSEVELT, JR.

afraid I might be trespassing, because he was there, all right. The room was crammed with books and pictures and memorabilia, but the lion rugs on the floor were the objects of our special affection. It was fun to lie on them and pretend they were alive. Grandmother used to read to us, generally from Howard Pyle's *Robin Hood* or something else by him, because Pyle was one of Grandfather's favorite authors, especially for reading to the children.

On the left was Grandmother's parlor, where we children were not permitted. She secluded herself there to read and did not like to be disturbed. It was a "withdrawing" room in the true sense of the word. She had an endless curiosity, and when, in her seventies, she did leave Sagamore, it was to go on long voyages all over the world. However, we children really did not mind being excluded from her drawing room, since it contained only one item of interest to us—a luxurious polar-bear skin that we sneaked onto now and then.

Farther down the hall, on the right, was the dining room, its door flanked by a large gong used to summon us to meals. It was always rung by Clara, the waitress, Grandmother's downstairs lieutenant. Clara was a distinguished-looking light-skinned Negro woman of a commanding authority that kept us in our place within her domain.

Grandfather definitely was with us at table. As in his lifetime, we consumed mounds of good food, running to rich, homemade soups and succulent roasts and always a delicious dessert. This last course was particularly exciting because of the importance of who got which doily under the finger bowl. There were only two that mattered—the red dragon was the best, but the green dragon was good, too. We often ate off dessert plates with holes around the sides and heard how our nearsighted grandfather used to pour the cream until it flowed through the holes and then look up guiltily to see if Grandmother had noticed. To us it was natural to suppose that he was a bit in awe of her himself.

The best times were the Christmas holidays, when all the family gathered to eat the great Christmas dinner, with its turkey and suckling pig that fathers and uncles vied with each other to carve. After lunch we would go through the pantry, admiring its archaic wooden icebox, to the huge kitchen to congratulate Bridget, the cook, a merry miniature of a woman with a lovely, lilting brogue.

Following this heavy meal we were sent upstairs to nap. The stairs themselves were in Stygian blackness, and we had to feel our way along. This caused much talk among our parents of the dangers of falling, but we children got a certain thrill from these dark, mysterious stairs. The second-floor hall surrounding the stairwell, which gave into the bedrooms, was equally dark and was hung with pictures of vaguely threatening ancestors. It took a bit of courage to cross this hall to the bathroom

during the night, especially when I looked at an ancestress known as "The Lady with Eyes." Her eyes followed me malevolently as I crept along guided only by a tallow light flickering on a table. (This had been placed there years ago for Uncle Quentin—the other ghost in the house—who as a small boy had been afraid of the dark. He was later killed in World War I.) Occasionally I had a nightmare in which that light slowly flickered out, leaving me in the dark hall alone!

There are ten bedrooms on that floor, counting Grandfather's dressing room, and as a child I slept in every one except, of course, the master bedroom. Each had a distinct character and history, as did the big bathroom that for a long time had been the only one in the house. Its huge antique tub stood magnificently on a pedestal, and the old-fashioned washbowls still sat in various spots, unused since Grandfather's day.

The ancient facilities of the house, commonplace to our parents, were a constant source of fascination. We discovered the speaking tubes, stuffed up with paper and no longer in use. We soon corrected that and for a day or two amused ourselves by exchanging messages from distant parts of the house until the tubes were stopped up again by a grandmotherly ukase. Then we found the dumbwaiter, used primarily to transport wood to the fireplaces on the upper floors. For us it turned out to be a delightful mode of transportation up and down, until we got a bad fright when cousin Quentin lost control of the pulleys and crashed to the cellar, shaking the whole house and thereby producing another ukase.

And best of all, at the end of a dark hall on the third floor, was the gun room. Here—amid shelves of books about exploration and big game and a large collection of guns—Grandfather came on strongest of all, especially at his desk, where he once looked out the window over a broad panorama of Long Island Sound. It was very much his room. Grandmother—and even our parents—almost never went up there, and our ghost very kindly did not object to our playing with his weapons. The prize one for use was a wonderful rusting six-shooter, and we played the sort of games that nowadays would not meet with general approval. I once came to grief acting out the part of a Chinese general. My prop was an old sword—possibly the one Grandfather used as a Rough Rider. Its scabbard had rotted, and when I drew it to charge, I nearly cut off my fingers.

We did not mind which bedroom was assigned to us, but our parents did. They complained of the hardness of the mattresses, especially that of one bed, which for its stoniness was known as "Pharaoh's Heart." But we could not tell the difference. I felt Grandfather particularly haunted two of the rooms. One was the bedroom in the southwest corner where he died, which had a bedspread designed as an American flag. So strongly did I sense his presence that I once had a conversation with him there in which I asked him to help me be worthy of him. He never answered, but I thought he might be listening. The other room was his small dressing room on the north side, where the wind, whistling eerily in the winter night, made it easy for spirits to return.

Oddly enough, I never felt his presence in the master bedroom. This was so much Grandmother's domain, with Irish Mary, the upstairs maid, hovering in the background. We would go in there only occasionally for a brief levee, when she would receive us after breakfast, sitting up in the massive double bed.

The largest room in the house, the North Room, was closed off and absolutely forbidden to us except on holidays. Grandfather had built this room to hold his game trophies and various presents from potentates all over the world, and to serve as a family feast room. We made the most of the rare occasions when we were allowed in. It was the most fascinating room of all, with its skins of lions and other beasts, two great bison heads over the fireplaces, and a pair of huge, splendid elephant tusks given him by the Emperor of Ethiopia. The ceiling was twenty feet high, and I remember the room as very cold, so that much of the time we huddled in front of a roaring fire in its wide fireplace. Once a year a tall Christmas tree was brought in, and after Christmas lunch the whole family would gather to collect their spoils. To me the most evocative thing in the room today is the Rough Rider's hat, thrown casually over the horns of an elk.

I haven't said anything about nostalgia or the sadness of his loss, but of course we all felt that. I always missed the grandfather I never really had. There is a picture of him beaming down on me as he held his latest grandchild in his arms [see page 73], but I was still far too young to know he was about to leave me. I used to feel saddest about this on the porch in the evening, sitting in an old rocking chair as he must have done, looking down over the broad fields toward the woods, listening to the katydids.

For his presence was almost as strong outside the house as in it. Outside the North Room we played on the cannon from the Spanish-American War, then tramped through the autumn leaves to the garage. This was the domain of Grandfather's genial black coachman, Charlie Lee. He was Clara's husband, and he now drove Grandmother's limousine for her trips to church and her other infrequent sallies away from Sagamore Hill.

I shall never forget the delights of Grandfather's farm, with its fruits and chickens and cows, to say nothing of the wonderful old barn where, burrowing through the hay, he used to play hide-and-go-seek with *his* children, just as our fathers did with us.

The fields were perfect for playing, and my father and uncles led us in the same strenuous games Grandfather

Teddy Roosevelt's grandson Archie—Archibald Bullock Roosevelt, Jr.—is a foreign service officer assigned to the State Department in Washington. And Sagamore Hill in Oyster Bay, New York, is now a national historic site. "Even though it is refurbished and roped off, it still does not feel quite like a museum," Mr. Roosevelt reports. "I visited Sagamore only the other day, and I still felt Grandfather there guarding his heritage."

had played with them. To work off a big meal, there was "shinny"—ground hockey, well named for the many blows borne by the shins. I remember a sort of blindman's buff we called "Still Pond No More Moving." One field was reserved for rifle practice, and all of us male children were taken there by our fathers to learn to shoot, just as their father had taught them.

Farther afield were other holiday pastimes of Grandfather's—the point-to-point walk, the paper-chase, and the run to the seashore down Cooper's Bluff. We were left in freedom in the lovely woods surrounding Sagamore, just made for children. Grandmother never ventured far, preferring the rose arbor, where she cut a Victorian figure, dressed in white chiffon, basket in hand, and accompanied by her aged, nasty-tempered little dog, Shady.

And then there was the beach. We walked down an overgrown path, passing through an orchard gone to seed—the "Fairy Apple Orchard"—where we could still see little gardens laid out by our parents when they were our age. Before we got to the beach, we passed a long, somewhat smelly salt-water creek, where we used to roll in the mud and chase fiddler crabs. We could also dig clams on the beach, or more exciting, seine for shiners, flounders, and eels. And we knew the joys of an old-fashioned picnic just as Grandfather had loved it—a nice bonfire, steak, and potatoes roasting in the coals, with plenty of sandwiches thrown in and a little sand in everything. At nighttime Grandfather used to tell ghost stories. My father inherited the talent, building up suspense by the tone of his voice, which grew lower and more ominous as the story reached its climax, until we all shivered in excitement and not a little fear. On those nights a susceptible younger sister would have nightmares, and Father would be reprimanded by Mother, as his father must have been before him—with just as little effect.

So, though I passed a youth without grandfathers—my other grandfather died at almost the same time—this was in the physical sense only. Actually my Sagamore Hill grandfather was with us all the time and enlivened our young lives with his gay spirit even after death. We never knew him except as a ghost—but what a merry, vital, and energetic ghost he was. And how much encouragement and strength he left behind to help us face the terrible half century that has passed since his death.

While three of his sons were at war (note the flag), T.R. posed at Sagamore Hill with his newest grandchild, author of this article. Watching fondly are, from left, Archie's mother, "Grandmother" Roosevelt, and "Auntie Ethel" Derby. The children are Richard and Edith Derby.

When shall we three meet again In thunder, lightning, or in rain?

Text by AVON NEAL, *photographs by* ANN PARKER

For years American folk art enthusiasts have been prowling inside attics and old barns to search out primitive objects from our creative past, yet all the time there has been another treasure outdoors, one often quite overlooked. It is the vast legion of imaginative folk figures that appear in our landscape as scarecrows, harvest figures, and snowmen, conceived in the best of folk art traditions. No two are alike; each projects its individual gesture and expression. And they rarely survive the season they are designed to celebrate. Every year tens of thousands of these fanciful effigies are manufactured by people totally unaware that they are participants in a contemporary, but seldom recorded, folk art tradition. The ones we show here are confined to New England, but others like them can be found almost anywhere.

Scarecrows are the most utilitarian of all this ephemeral clan. They are also the most romantic. From time immemorial these ragged apparitions have inspired poets, storytellers, and artists; they have graced the pages of literature from the Bible to Chaucer's tales and La Fontaine's fables, through Hawthorne's stories right down to *The Wizard of Oz*. They are basically spontaneous, hastily improvised affairs that demonstrate the boundless ingenuity that can be embodied in a couple of sticks and a few old clothes.

The American scarecrow had its heyday in the latter part of the nineteenth century. It cut such a figure of sartorial elegance among the corn rows that tales of tramps exchanging their worn-out wardrobes for the scarecrow's finer garb became legendary. Since then the art of scarecrow making has declined appreciably, depending more on working clothes and such pop art accouterments as aluminum pie tins held dangling in the wind. There was a time in America when no rustic scene would have seemed complete without some representation of this spectral image standing guard among the farmer's crops, but they are rare today. Science now has more effective ways of discouraging marauding crows.

Harvest figures are gaudier manifestations of the common man's creative urge. Their leaf-filled bodies and grotesque features carved from pumpkins or painted on paper bags are designed to celebrate Halloween and the autumn festival. Although they are comparative newcomers to the folk figure scene they have historic precedents in Old World superstitions and religious customs. Theirs is the eerie domain of warlocks and witches, of goblins and ghosts, of pagan gods and fairy folk, and of all those capricious spirits who cavort in October's nocturnal revels. Since they are usually made by children, it is not surprising that these lighthearted figures are the most colorful and uninhibited members of the folk figure family.

Snowmen are the sand castles of an inclement season, and they are as fleeting as childhood itself. Winter provides the first real opportunity for young artists to make life-sized figures from a commonplace material, and they happily populate snowy landscapes with their sculptured images. Most are simple constructions, but a few are truly inspired and exhibit a bold imagination in the use of adornment that often transforms the lowliest snowman into a monument of artistic beauty.

Scarecrow, harvest figure, snowman—they are all creatures of whim and circumstance. They are provocative. They are at once beautiful and ridiculous. And they satisfy the inherent urge in all mankind to portray the human form, whether for artistic or utilitarian purposes. It is probable that these colorful but unsophisticated figures, however transient, provide some of the most expressive folk art of our time.

On these two pages are one example each of ephemeral folk figures: a harvest cut-out on a door near New Braintree, Massachusetts; a snowman of gentle mien from the Sturbridge area; and a windblown scarecrow surrounded by poppies in southern Vermont.

The Massachusetts harvest figures on this page include a wizard with a rubber mask (top) from Palmer, a pumpkin hero from North Brookfield, and a stuffed witch with a paper face from Leicester. On the facing page are scarecrows in various stages of decrepitude. There is a Dick Tracy look to the pot-head at top, and genial idiocy suffuses the aspect of the watcher over the corn at center, photographed in the little town of Harvard, Massachusetts. The saddest sight is the threadbare remainder of the scarecrow at bottom as winter comes on in the garden of our authors at North Brookfield, Massachusetts.

Avon Neal and his wife, Ann Parker, are artists and extensive travellers who have recently brought out a book called Ephemeral Folk Figures, *published by Clarkson N. Potter, New York. An exhibit that includes their pictures and several actual scarecrows is now showing at the Museum of American Folk Art in New York, and will move in early summer to the Albany (New York) Institute of History and Art, and in midwinter to the Amon Carter Museum of Western Art in Fort Worth, Texas. The Neals are also known for their rubbings of early American gravestones, some of which will appear soon in this magazine.*

Ida Minerva Tarbell hardly resembled her public image as the nemesis of the world's most powerful tycoon.

The *Gentlewoman* and the
ROBBER BARON

By VIRGINIA VAN DER VEER HAMILTON

One wintry morning in 1902 a prim, resolute spinster presented herself at 26 Broadway in New York City, bastion of the powerful Standard Oil organization. Promptly she was ushered through a maze of empty corridors to a reception room facing an open courtyard. As she waited, she became aware that a man in a nearby window was observing her stealthily.

Over the next two years this unlikely visitor paid many calls to one of the most awesome addresses in the American financial world. Each time she saw only the clerks who guided her, a secretary, and Henry H. Rogers, vice president of Standard Oil. But always she noticed the same shadowy figure watching her from the window. Was John D. Rockefeller, master of the oil industry, peeping at Ida Minerva Tarbell, lady journalist?

If so, Ida's turn to peep came one Sunday in 1903 when she visited the Euclid Avenue Baptist Church in Cleveland. Feeling a little guilty about it, she had invaded Rockefeller's church for a firsthand look at the man whose business practices she dared to castigate. Her quarry soon appeared. At sixty-four Rockefeller exuded power, but Ida observed that his big head had a wet look, his nose resembled a sharp thorn, and his lips

were thin slits. Constantly, uneasily, Rockefeller peered around the familiar congregation, but if he recognized the stranger in its midst, he gave no sign.

Although the nation's richest man and his most persistent critic never met, their confrontation in the pages of *McClure's Magazine* enthralled thousands of Americans. Safe within their Victorian mansions, well-bred ladies shuddered at the audacity of one of their sex who had the spunk to describe the legendary Rockefeller as cold, ruthless, and unethical.

For eighteen installments—from November, 1902, to April, 1904—Ida's monumental "History of the Standard Oil Company" fired the indignation of middle-aged and middle-class citizens caught up in the rebellious mood of Progressivism. Politicians from statehouse legislators to Teddy Roosevelt at the White House took note of the furor. Its echoes eventually penetrated even the remote chambers of the Supreme Court.

Readers of *McClure's*, turning through their October, 1902, issue, were introduced to the sensational serial by a full-page photograph of Ida. The magazine's star writer wore a severe, high-collared white dress adorned with tucks and embroidery, and her dark hair was piled high

Judge, 1904: CULVER PICTURES

The anti-Rockefeller furor stirred up by Miss Tarbell's "History of the Standard Oil Company" is evident in this cartoon, in which the magazine Judge *is asking the ink-slinging muckrakers, "Boys, don't you think you have bothered the old man just about enough?"*

on her head. She looked away from the camera with an air of cool detachment. Miss Tarbell, *McClure's* announced, had completed her long study of "the most perfectly developed trust in existence." Her account would begin the following month.

S. S. McClure, impulsive and mercurial, boasted that the founding of *McClure's* and the discovery of Ida Tarbell were his proudest achievements. In Paris in 1892 he had bounded up four flights of steps to an apartment to meet the little-known American writer. After pouring out his plans for *McClure's*, S. S. borrowed forty dollars and left. "I'll never see that money," Ida lamented, but to her relief the forty dollars was promptly repaid. Two years later Ida, serious, purposeful, and thirty-seven, joined the staff of *McClure's* in New York.

S. S. soon had reason to congratulate himself. Ida was an immediate hit with readers, who paid ten cents a copy for his lively magazine. They liked her biography of Napoleon, produced "on the gallop" in six weeks. They followed with avid interest her series on Abraham Lincoln, written after four years of painstaking research in Kentucky, Indiana, and Illinois.

As thousands of new subscribers joined his circulation

lists, McClure gave Ida most of the credit. The life of Lincoln, he said, "told on our circulation as nothing ever had before." By 1900 *McClure's* was reaching 350,000 homes and was second in circulation only to its bitter rival, *Munsey's*. If McClure liked an idea, he bragged, then millions of readers would like it, too. "There's only one better editor than I am," he admitted, "and that's Frank Munsey. If he likes a thing, then everybody will like it."

Alert to the mood of his readers, McClure sensed their concern about social and political reform. Lincoln Steffens, therefore, must check into corruption in the big cities. Ray Stannard Baker must investigate labor unions and the coal strike then going on in the anthracite fields of Pennsylvania (see "The Coal Kings Come to Judgment" in the April, 1960, AMERICAN HERITAGE). As for Ida, why not a study of one of the monopolies that frightened small businessmen? Why not, in fact, the prototype of them all? "Out with you!" S. S. commanded his talented staff. "Look, see, report."

"Don't do it, Ida," her father pleaded. "They will ruin the magazine." Others warned her of the "all-seeing eye and the all-powerful reach" of Standard Oil. If *McClure's* persisted, friends predicted, "they'll get you in the end."

Standard Oil was well aware that a popular journalist —and a female at that—was prying into its past. Executives of the corporation asked no less a public figure than Mark Twain to inquire what *McClure's* planned to publish. "You will have to ask Miss Tarbell," S. S. replied. "Would Miss Tarbell see Mr. Rogers?" Twain inquired. When her supporters heard that Ida was visiting 26 Broadway to get the company's side of its history, they were instantly suspicious. "You'll become their apologist before you get through," many prophesied.

At their first meeting Ida and Henry Rogers discovered that they had been neighbors years before in the booming oil regions of Pennsylvania, where Ida's father had made tanks and Rogers had been an independent refiner. They even recalled the beauty of a wooded ravine separating their houses. Although she decided that Henry Rogers was "as fine a pirate as ever flew his flag in Wall Street," Ida was not beguiled by nostalgic memories. She alone, she told the Standard Oil executive, would be the judge of what she wrote.

Diligent and methodical, Ida studied musty records of the many lawsuits brought against Standard Oil in the thirty years since its incorporation. Every pertinent document must be located: "somewhere, some time," Ida insisted, "a copy turns up." Rogers once suggested that Ida should meet Rockefeller himself, and somewhat apprehensively she agreed. But their meeting was never arranged.

Seeking firsthand knowledge of Standard's methods, Ida interviewed other businessmen. Reluctant though they might be, they usually responded to her firm, dignified manner. One eccentric Cleveland millionaire received her with his hat on, his feet propped on his desk, and his face buried in a newspaper. As Ida quietly began to ask questions, he placed his feet on the floor, put down the newspaper, removed his hat, and gave her his respectful attention.

Her first installment was a vivid account of the brawling, gambling spirit of pioneer days in the Pennsylvania oil country. In 1859, when they heard the exhilarating news that oil was gushing out of a well near Titusville, thousands of adventurous Americans poured into the area, and a whole series of boom towns—with names like Pit Hole, Oil City, Petroleum Center, and Rouseville —hastily sprang up. "On every rocky farm," Ida wrote, "in every poor settlement of the region, was some man whose ear was attuned to Fortune's call, and who had the daring and the energy to risk everything he possessed in an oil lease." Saloons, brothels, and dance halls catered to a drifting population of fortune seekers.

Recalling the atmosphere of her youth, Ida praised the efforts of many citizens of this rough frontier to create schools, churches, and a proper environment. Her own parents, Esther and Franklin Tarbell, had shep-

herded their children into respectable middle-class ways, highlighted by family picnics on Chautauqua Lake or an occasional trip to Cleveland. Crusading suffragettes visited the Tarbell home, and young Ida fell under the spell of their fervent talk. "I must be free," she vowed, "and to be free I must be a spinster." At fourteen she prayed on her knees that God would keep her from marriage.

To prepare for a career, Ida entered Allegheny College at Meadville, the lone girl in a freshman class of forty "hostile or indifferent" boys. After graduation she hoped to become a biologist, but fate and S. S. McClure decided otherwise. Now, twenty-two years later, this child of the oil regions who had elected spinsterhood and freedom was challenging the ruler of the oil industry himself.

At the close of the first chapter Ida offered her readers an enticing glimpse of the drama to come. Praising the independent oil producers, who gambled their lives and money in an uncertain new industry, she wrote:

Life ran swift and ruddy and joyous in these men. They were still young, most of them under forty, and they looked forward with all the eagerness of the young who have just learned their powers, to years of struggle and development. . . . There was nothing too good for them, nothing they did not hope and dare. But suddenly, at the very heyday of this confidence, a big hand reached out from nobody knew where, to steal their conquest and throttle their future.

The "big hand," she revealed in her next installment, was an enterprising young man with "remarkable commercial vision, a genius for seeing the possibilities in material things." As a boy of thirteen John Rockefeller discovered that lending money at 7 per cent interest was more profitable than his earlier job of digging potatoes: "It was a good thing," the boy reasoned, "to let the money be my slave." This principle, Ida told her readers, was the foundation of a great financial career.

During the Civil War, Rockefeller chose to sell produce to the Union army rather than to serve in its ranks. Before the war ended, the twenty-three-year-old merchant had foreseen greater potential in refining a new product, oil, to light the homes and lubricate the machines of America. Under his shrewd and frugal leadership his first refinery prospered. There must be no waste, Rockefeller decreed. He found a market even for the residuum that other refineries allowed to flow away into the ground. "It hurt him to see it unused," Ida wrote, "and no man had a heartier welcome from the president of the Standard Oil Company than he who would show him how to utilize any proportion of his residuum." Rather than pay a barrelmaker, Rockefeller set up his own barrel factory.

The youthful refiner got his greatest joy from a good bargain. One of those whom Ida interviewed told her that the only time he had ever seen Rockefeller enthusiastic was at the news that his firm had bought a cargo of oil much below the market price. "He bounded from his chair with a shout of joy," the man recollected, "danced up and down, hugged me, threw up his hat, acted so like a madman that I have never forgotten it."

On the basis of the large amount of oil he shipped eastward, Rockefeller began to receive the railroad rebates that Ida charged were the keystone of his future empire. She described how he and other large refiners conspired to force railroads to grant them "drawbacks," additional rebates on the shipments of their competitors. Members of this clandestine combination, known as the South Improvement Company, received a rebate of $1.06 a barrel on crude oil shipped from Cleveland to New York, plus a drawback of $1.06 on each barrel shipped by their rivals. When an independent refiner paid eighty cents a barrel to ship crude oil from the Pennsylvania fields to Cleveland, the South Improvement Company received a forty-cent-per-barrel drawback on the shipment.

This advantage, Ida charged, was used as a club over the heads of other refiners in Cleveland, forcing them to "sell or perish." His competitors wanted to keep their own businesses, Ida said, but "Mr. Rockefeller was regretful but firm. It was useless to resist, he told the hesitating; they would certainly be crushed if they did not accept his offer." When twenty-one of the twenty-six firms sold out to Rockefeller, he controlled one fifth of the nation's oil refining; "almost the entire independent oil interests of Cleveland collapsed in three months' time," Ida informed her readers. Privately an indignant Rockefeller denied Ida's version. Standard had been an angel of mercy to the Cleveland firms in distress, he told friends. "They didn't collapse," he insisted. "They had collapsed before! That's the reason they were so glad to combine their interest with ours, or take the money we offered." However, Rockefeller, who had always met criticism with lofty silence, refused to reply publicly to the articles in *McClure's*. "Not a word," he insisted. "Not a word about that misguided woman!"

But the heir to Standard Oil, John D. Rockefeller, Jr., was stung to a veiled defense of his father's business creation. In a speech entitled "Christianity and Business" he told members of the Y.M.C.A. at his alma mater, Brown University: "The American Beauty rose can be produced in its splendor and fragrance only by sacrificing the early buds which grow up around it." Critics of Standard Oil never let John D., Jr., forget this unfortunate metaphor. Recalling it several years later, a bishop declared from the pulpit: "A rose by any other name will smell as sweet, but the odor of that rose to me smacks strongly of crude petroleum."

If the creation of a perfect rose justified the sacrifice of other buds, could the same rationale be applied to the Standard Oil Trust? Ida's answer was a vehement No.

The heroes of her serial were the independent oil "farmers" and refiners whose livelihood was threatened by Rockefeller's growing consolidation. "They believed," Ida wrote, "in independent effort—every man for himself and fair play for all. They wanted competition, loved open fight. They considered that all business should be done openly; that the railways were bound as public carriers to give equal rates; that any combination which favoured one firm or one locality at the expense of another was unjust and illegal."

The producers rose in united revolt against the South Improvement Company and the man whom they believed

Ida's articles disturbed John D. Rockefeller, Jr., who defended the Standard as a "rose [that] can be produced . . . only by sacrificing the early buds which grow up around it." Angry reactions included this cartoon showing the "buds" at the feet of the senior Rockefeller as the skulls of competitors whom he had crushed.

to be its Mephistopheles, refusing to sell oil until railroads agreed not to grant rebates, drawbacks, or any other special privileges. Ida remembered vividly that her own father, by then a producer himself, was one of those who had pledged not to sell.

The South Improvement Company scheme was defeated, but Rockefeller, Ida said, "had a mind which stopped by a wall, burrows under or creeps around." He next negotiated a new rebate arrangement between Standard Oil and the New York Central Railroad. In a burst of indignant prose Ida berated her protagonist:

There was no more faithful Baptist in Cleveland than he. Every enterprise of that church he had supported liberally from his youth. He gave to its poor. He visited its sick. He wept with its suffering. Moreover, he gave unostentatiously to many outside charities of whose worthiness he was satisfied. He was simple and frugal in his habits. He never went to the theatre, never drank wine. He gave much time to the training of his children, seeking to develop in them his own habits of economy and charity. Yet he was willing to strain every nerve to obtain for himself special and unjust privileges from the railroads which were bound to ruin every man in the oil business not sharing them with him.

Rockefeller's next tactic, Ida explained, was to form a national Refiners' Association to force oil producers to sell their output to a united front of refiners. To offset

Ida's "History" helped launch an investigation of the Standard by the Bureau of Corporations in 1905–6. Its final report, given to President Theodore Roosevelt by the bureau's chief, James R. Garfield (a son of the assassinated President), called for antitrust action. Along with the Standard's Henry H. Rogers, who up to a point had co-operated with Ida, Rockefeller was glum.

the power of the refiners, drillers organized a Producers' Association. The producers realized that overproduction was their curse. If they agreed to stop drilling new wells for six months and shut down their pumps for thirty days, supplies of crude oil would dwindle, and prices would rise. To the producers' surprise, Rockefeller and his fellow refiners offered them a contract for 200,000

barrels of oil at $3.25 a barrel. They signed. But when 50,000 of the 200,000 barrels had been shipped, the refiners' association broke its contract, declaring that the producers had failed to limit production and that plenty of oil was available at $2.50 a barrel. Ida placed the blame on Rockefeller for "leading them into an alliance, and at the psychological moment throwing up his contract."

One producer told Ida what it had been like to negotiate with Rockefeller, who during one meeting sat and rocked with his hands covering his eyes.

I made a speech which I guess was pretty warlike. Well, right in the middle of it, John Rockefeller stopped rocking and took down his hands and looked at me. You never saw such eyes. He took me all in, saw just how much fight he could expect from me, and I knew it, and then up went his hands and back and forth went his chair.

Month by month Ida pressed her indictment, picturing Rockefeller as a sinister conspirator obsessed with a passion to control the entire oil industry for the "holy blue barrel," as his competitors called it, of Standard Oil. He arranged for Standard to receive even more favorable rebates from major railroads. When independent operators developed a revolutionary new means of transporting oil by pipelines, the canny Rockefeller realized that this method was the shipping trend of the future. He moved into the pipeline business, driving out rivals until he controlled the entire pipeline system of the oil regions. He set up a nationwide network, paying spies to report on rival shipments, deliberately underselling his competitors, and then, having driven his rivals out of a territory, set any price he pleased.

Summarizing Rockefeller's goal, Ida wrote:

Briefly stated, his argument was this: "Controlling all refineries, I shall be the only shipper of oil. Being the only shipper, I can obtain special rates of transportation which will drive out and keep out competitors; controlling all refineries, I shall be the only buyer, and can regulate the price of crude [oil] as I can the price of refined."

The charge of spying, published in a chapter titled "Cutting to Kill," abruptly ended Ida's harmonious interviews with Henry Rogers. To substantiate her charges, *McClure's* reproduced records sent to Ida secretly by a young shipping clerk in a Standard plant. They were undercover reports from railroad agents, listing oil shipments by rival producers. On her next visit to 26 Broadway, Ida found Rogers "by no means cordial." When he asked where she got "that stuff," she replied boldly: "You know very well that I could not tell you where I got that stuff, but you know very well that it is authentic." It was their last interview.

Although the doors of Standard Oil closed to Ida, she was invited to meet an even more unexpected source of information. Frank Rockefeller summoned her secretly to Cleveland to hear his grievances against his successful brother. To help finance a shipping business, Frank had borrowed money from John D. and put up his Standard Oil stock as collateral. During the Panic of '93, when Frank was unable to meet his obligations, John D. foreclosed and took over the stock. Frank, observed Ida, was more frivolous than his brother, more generous, "not a safe man to handle money. . . . So it was a kind of obligation to the sacredness of money," she wrote, "that John Rockefeller had foreclosed on his own brother."

After chastising Rockefeller for many months, Ida produced an installment called "The Legitimate Greatness of the Standard Oil Company" in which she freely acknowledged its leader's business efficiency. Rockefeller's passion for detail and for plowing profits back into the company, she said, had resulted in a masterpiece of organization. Even the dust on the floors of his tin factories was sifted to save filings and bits of solder.

While granting Rockefeller his due, Ida could not forgive practices she considered illegitimate and debasing to business morality. His success, she feared, would tempt thousands of others to "Commercial Machiavellianism." In the wake of his growing monopoly, Ida said, Rockefeller left a trail of devastated small businesses:

Why one should love an oil refinery the outsider may not see, but to the man who had begun with one still and had seen it grow by his own energy and intelligence to ten, who now sold 500 barrels a day where he once sold five, the refinery was the dearest spot on earth save his home. . . . To ask such a man to give up his refinery was to ask him to give up the thing which, after his family, meant most in life to him.

But faced with the growing power of Standard Oil, the independents did give up. Describing one who sold out, Ida wrote that "he realized that something . . . was at work in the oil business—something resistless, silent, perfect in its might—and he sold out to that something." Along Oil Creek, she said, "the little refineries which for years had faced every difficulty with stout hearts collapsed. 'Sold out,' 'dismantled,' 'shut down,' is the melancholy record."

As dramatic proof of the fierceness of the conflict Ida devoted an entire installment to "The Buffalo Case," in which managers of a Standard affiliate in New York were convicted of conspiring to blow up a rival refinery to force it out of business. In another chapter she shocked her public by repeating the tale of Widow Backus, who declared in an affidavit that Rockefeller had fleeced her of a fair price when she sold her husband's refinery to Standard Oil. Ida said of the widow:

She had seen every effort to preserve an independent business thwarted. Rightly or wrongly, she had come to believe that a refusal to sell meant a fight with Mr. Rockefeller, that a fight meant ultimately defeat, and she gave up her business to avoid ruin.

Historians later criticized Ida for repeating the widow's tale, which was of questionable accuracy, but true or exaggerated, it made a sensational installment. Victorian ladies of comfortable means could identify with the plight of Widow Backus.

Acknowledged as "Lord of the Oil Regions" by 1879, Rockefeller controlled 90 per cent of the oil business of the nation, dominating refining, transporting, and marketing. The entire pipeline system of the Pennsylvania fields belonged to Standard. Rockefeller had achieved his goal, Ida wrote, "because he had the essential element to all great achievement, a steadfastness to purpose once conceived which nothing can crush."

To handle the affairs of his giant monopoly, Rockefeller created a new type of business organization, the trust, whereby he and eight other trustees managed the entire structure. But public resentment against the monopoly began to be reflected in a rash of legal suits. Ida reminded her readers of the 1892 ruling by the supreme court of Ohio that had resulted in dissolution of the Standard Oil Trust. It was replaced by the Standard Oil Company of New Jersey, which functioned as a holding company for the Rockefeller interests.

After eighteen chapters and almost four years of research and writing Ida and *McClure's* rested their case against John D. Rockefeller. Summing it all up, Ida told her faithful readers that they were paying more for oil under monopoly conditions than they would pay under free competition. Business opportunity in the oil industry, she said, was now limited to a few hundred men.

But there was a more serious side to it, she concluded. The ethical cost of all this should be a deep concern. "Canonize 'business success,' and men who make a success like that of the Standard Oil Trust become national heroes!" Defenders of Rockefeller might justify his methods by saying, "It's business" or "All humans are erring mortals," but Ida would not accept a moral code that "would leave our business men weeping on one another's shoulders over human frailty, while they picked one another's pockets."

In a last plea to her readers she urged them to ostracize monopolists who used unethical practices as they would ostracize unethical doctors, lawyers, or athletes, for "a thing won by breaking the rules of the game," she moralized, "is not worth the winning."

As her public exploded with wrath, *McClure's* was deluged with angry letters. Ida, readers said, was a modern Joan of Arc and "the Terror of the Trusts." Her study reminded one man of "the clarion notes of the old prophets of Israel." Another called it "the *Uncle Tom's Cabin* of today." A letter addressed to "Ida M. Tarbell, Rockefeller Station, Hades," reached her promptly.

McClure's, packed with articles by Steffens and Baker as well as with Ida's literary dynamite, thrived on its crusading zeal. But Ida was even more of a celebrity than her colleagues, and they joined in the general admiration for her work. "Ida Tarbell was the best of us," Baker admitted. In a western city a newspaper hailed the arrival of William Allen White and Ida with the headline "Celebrated Writers Here." S. S. wrote his protégée: "You are today the most generally famous woman in America."

Ida's "History" evoked even more praise when it was published as a two-volume book in 1904. "Miss Tarbell,"

John D.

Gov. Hoch of Kansas

Thomas W. Lawson

Miss Ida Tarbell of McClure's Magazine

The Standard Oil Company has never violated the law. The Standard Oil Company has no connection, direct or indirect, with the organization of any gas or copper Company

When, after the "History" appeared, Standard Oil moved in on new wells in Kansas, Kansans fought back, with a reluctant Ida as their champion. Here Rockefeller defends his policies—to the disbelief of Ida, the governor of Kansas, and Thomas W. Lawson, a muckraker of Wall Street.

said the Cleveland *Leader*, "has done more to dethrone Rockefeller in public esteem than all the preachers in the land." The New York *News* declared that "Rockefeller's very conscience is exposed by her search for truth." The Norfolk *Dispatch* and the Washington *News* proclaimed Ida "a great woman historian" and "probably the most talented woman writer of history that this country has produced."

Standard, however, was not without its defenders. In Pennsylvania the Oil City *Derrick*, subsidized by the company, headlined its review: "Hysterical Woman Versus Historical Facts." A Harvard economist, Gilbert Montague, who wrote a sympathetic history of Standard's operations, termed Ida "a mere gatherer of folklore." The popular essayist Elbert Hubbard said Standard Oil was an example of "survival of the fittest" and called Ida a "literary bushwhacker" who "shot from cover and . . . shot to kill." The nickname Miss Tarbarrel was coined

by Standard supporters. Even Rockefeller himself, not a notably humorous man, adopted the pun with glee.

While interest in Ida's history was at its height, new oil discoveries by wildcatters drilling deep in the Kansas plains caused a fresh boom. Standard Oil moved quickly into the new fields, threading its pipelines across prairie and farmland. But *McClure's* had reached even the remote farmers of Kansas. Populists, women's clubs, and independent oilmen vowed to keep Standard out of their fields even if they had to set up a state-owned refinery in the penitentiary. At the urging of the oilmen Ida visited the new arena. To her dismay she was received as a prophet and serenaded by oil boomers. "But here I was," she wrote later, "fifty, fagged, wanting to be let alone while I collected trustworthy information for my articles—dragged to the front as an apostle."

The news from Kansas, added to the cumulative effect of the Tarbell series, helped stir Congress to action. In February, 1905, it authorized the Bureau of Corporations to investigate the low price of crude oil, particularly in Kansas. Could the wide margin between the prices of crude and refined, a Kansas congressman asked, be attributed to the operations of a trust or conspiracy?

Enthusiastically the Bureau of Corporations dug into its assignment. In the first of three lengthy reports to Congress, it concluded that Standard "habitually" received and was still receiving secret rebates and other "unjust and illegal discriminations" from railroads. The second report charged that Standard controlled the only major pipeline serving the oil industry and that it fought would-be competitors with lawsuits, right-of-way disputes, aid to railroads, and price wars. The final report accused Standard of keeping oil prices artificially high at the expense of the American consumer. Commissioner Herbert Knox Smith called for prosecution of Standard under the Sherman Antitrust Act.

The bureau's findings were not news to Ida's readers. One cartoonist pictured President Roosevelt receiving the reports on a slate bearing these words: "Standard Oil is just as naughty as Ida said it was." In the background of the cartoon was Henry Rogers, muttering to Rockefeller: "And I had my fingers crossed too."

But Roosevelt, who had originally encouraged federal legal action against Standard, became exasperated at the public vogue for the literature of exposure as other magazines and writers rushed to copy *McClure's* successful formula. Shortly after the appearance of an article in *Cosmopolitan* titled "The Treason of the Senate" an angry Roosevelt applied the term "muckrakers" to responsible and irresponsible journalists alike. Pondering the President's attack years later, Ida decided that Teddy preferred to conduct trust busting on his own and resented writers "stealing his thunder."

Meanwhile, Standard's troubles were multiplying. Three antitrust suits were brought against the corporation in state courts in 1904, four in 1905, and fourteen in 1906. Many resulted in fines or the temporary ouster of Standard from a state. The most sensational fine, $29,240,000 for 1,462 violations of the Elkins Act forbidding acceptance of rebates, was handed down by Judge Kenesaw Mountain Landis in August, 1907. Although this decision was later reversed, the "Big Fine" made Judge Landis famous and added drama to the controversy.

Once when Ida was searching for material in Indiana and Ohio, an order went out from Standard headquarters: "Simply ignore her entirely." But in the face of such mounting hostility even Standard Oil could not play the sphinx forever. The company began to give out information on its operations and employed Ivy Ledbetter Lee, an early public relations counsel, to place advertisements and friendly stories in newspapers and magazines. It ordered five thousand copies of Montague's book and distributed them to employees, ministers, libraries, teachers, and prominent citizens.

Rockefeller's own image was under such attack that a group of Congregational ministers balked at accepting his gift of $100,000 to their board of missions, calling it "tainted money." Later, to their embarrassment, they found that some of their colleagues had actually requested the gift. But the term "tainted money" briefly captured many a headline. Undeterred, Rockefeller intensified his long habit of philanthropy. Two months after the final chapter of the Standard Oil history appeared in *McClure's*, he announced gifts of one million dollars to Yale University and ten times that amount to the General Education Board, a philanthropy in aid of higher education that he had helped to establish two years before. No one objected. Such sums, the New York *Sun* commented dryly, "deodorize themselves." When it was charged that Rockefeller was using philanthropy to silence criticism, Ida came to his defense, reminding critics that Rockefeller had been a steady giver to church and charity since boyhood. If his gifts were larger now, she pointed out, it was because his income was greater and perhaps because he sought to call public attention to the benefits reaped from Standard Oil.

John D. proved his own most effective advocate. In 1909 he published a slim book titled *Random Reminiscences of Men and Events.* Although he did not mention Ida or other critics by name, it was obvious the outcry was on Rockefeller's mind. "Just how far one is justified . . . in defending himself from attacks is a moot point," he wrote. *Random Reminiscences,* an informal account of the early career, principles, and recreations of the nation's richest man, also contained useful hints on how to give money away wisely. This little book, one Rockefeller biographer has said, "did more to make Rockefeller a human figure than tons of Sunday supplement articles."

Random Reminiscences, however, did not persuade the federal government to call off a suit charging Standard Oil with violation of the Sherman act. The case dragged through three and a half years of litigation. In 1909 a federal circuit court sustained the government's position, but Standard appealed to the Supreme Court. Many an editor invited Ida to analyze the testimony. "I could have made a good killing out of that long investigation . . ." she recalled later. "But I had no stomach for it." Weary of all the controversy, she wished only "to escape into the safe retreat of a library where I could study people long dead."

Finally, on May 15, 1911, the decision was handed down. The highest court in the land declared Standard Oil of New Jersey to be a monopoly in restraint of trade, based on unfair practices. Charging that Standard's object was "to drive others from the field and exclude them from their right to trade," the court ordered the holding company dissolved. The justices, in effect, agreed with Ida.

"The History of the Standard Oil Company" was probably the most sensational serial ever to appear in an American magazine. Allan Nevins, in his biography of Rockefeller, called it "the most spectacular success of the muckraking school of journalism, and its most enduring achievement." As a historian Ida Tarbell had her flaws. She was untrained in economics. She yearned to turn back the clock to an era of individualism in business. She was obviously partial to independent oilmen, even though she scolded them for lacking the patience and fortitude to organize effectively against Rockefeller. In her indignation she sometimes exaggerated the iniquity of her archvillain.

But at a time when strong men quailed before the Rockefeller reputation, this daughter of the oil regions, fortified by her sense of righteous morality, boldly voiced their feelings. Although small operators lost their struggle for existence, Ida carried the day in the contest for public opinion. A modern-day historian of the muckraking era, David M. Chalmers, believes the image she fashioned of Rockefeller as a "cunning, ruthless Shylock" has not been successfully erased by a half century of Rockefeller family philanthropy. Forty years after her serial appeared, *Time* magazine credited the *McClure's* articles with bringing in a "gusher of public resentment that flowed all the way to the U. S. Supreme Court."

Was Ida's study an accurate work of historical research, or was it a subjective attack on practices of which she disapproved? Modern business historians, looking back on the "History" with the hindsight of a later era, generally substantiate her charges that Standard Oil built its monopoly upon special favors from railroads, mastery of the pipeline system, and sharp marketing

A victorious Ida Tarbell reading a pleasant headline

practices, all of which helped force small independents out of the fields and refineries.

But Ida raised a larger question: Was it better for the American oil industry to have free, albeit cutthroat, competition, or to fall under the dominance of a monopoly with the power to maintain orderly production and a profitable, if higher, price structure? It is this aspect of her account that still arouses controversy. Social historians tend to be on Ida's side, business historians to defend Rockefeller; both schools agree, however, that Ida was a pioneer business historian and that, although she worked with the crude research tools of the early 1900's and became a special pleader for her own moralistic ideas of business ethics, she presented a remarkably clear and truthful picture of the rise of Standard Oil.

Though John D. Rockefeller never met the stern

spinster who judged his business morality so harshly, she and Rockefeller's son, John D., Jr., did meet at a conference called by President Wilson after World War I. The younger Rockefeller, who had once compared Standard Oil to an American Beauty rose, had become disenchanted and had made "one of the most important decisions of my life." Resigning his directorships in Standard Oil and U. S. Steel, he announced in 1910 that he would devote his life to giving away the immense sums of money that flowed from his father's business creation.

When John D., Jr., realized he was to meet Ida, he sought the advice of William Allen White. The famous Kansas editor knew the younger Rockefeller as a gentle and kindhearted person for whom Ida's book had been "an unpleasant fact which gave him something more than pause." He advised Rockefeller to meet Miss Tarbell casually and naturally; as two sensitive people they would bridge the awkward situation. After the meeting White saw John D., Jr., hurrying into the street to hail a cab for Miss Tarbell. Later he was amused to see them, placed together by some inspired host at a formal dinner, "chatting amiably . . . each trying to outdo the other in politeness."

Although Ida wrote many other books and articles, none of her later works had the impact of the Standard Oil history. In 1922 she tried to revive her interest and write a third volume on Standard. But the fire and the burning indignation that had caught a nation's attention were gone. "Repeating yourself," she decided, "is a doubtful practice."

In 1937, as Ida at eighty was writing her autobiography, John D. Rockefeller died at the age of ninety-seven. The lady who had been his nemesis lived seven more years, enjoying the tranquillity of her Connecticut farm, where she made jelly and raised peonies, lettuce, and potatoes. An interviewer who sought her out in this retreat found her characteristically self-effacing: "The proof that I am able to do anything so worthwhile as raise a potato never fails to thrill me," said the Terror of the Trusts.

Dr. Virginia Van der Veer Hamilton is an assistant professor of history at the University of Alabama in Birmingham. She wrote "Hugo Black and the K.K.K." for our April, 1968, issue and is now completing a full-length biography of Mr. Justice Black.

For further reading: Success Story: The Life and Times of S. S. McClure, *by Peter Lyon (Scribner, 1963);* John D. Rockefeller: A Study in Power, *by Allan Nevins (2 volumes, Scribner, 1940);* All In the Day's Work, *the autobiography of Ida M. Tarbell (Macmillan, 1939);* The History of the Standard Oil Company, *by Ida M. Tarbell, abridged and with an introduction by David M. Chalmers (Harper Torchbooks, 1966).*

The Spies Who Came in from the Sea CONTINUED FROM PAGE 69

Dasch then indulged in a period of dawdling that he later explained was motivated by the conviction that the other six saboteurs should be given their own opportunity to save their skins by surrender. It was not until Thursday afternoon that Dasch boarded a train for Washington, still determined to see Hoover personally. He checked into Room 351 in the Mayflower Hotel.

On Friday morning, June 19, he telephoned the F.B.I. and was connected with Agent Duane L. Traynor. He must talk with Mr. Hoover, he said, finally disclosing that he was the leader of a group of German saboteurs. Traynor, who knew of the discovery of explosives at Amagansett and the hunt for the missing men, told Dasch firmly to stay right there in Room 351. Dasch did. A group of agents arrived with almost miraculous speed and escorted him to headquarters at the Department of Justice. Here, when he became persuaded that Hoover was not at leisure, he told his story to others. He gave them his handkerchief with the invisible writing. He jolted them with the news that there was a second sabotage group slated to land with explosives at Ponte Vedra Beach, Florida. They were to take two years, he said, to complete their work of destruction. Their major objectives were centered most heavily on aluminum production, transportation, and power stations.

The ingenious bombs masquerading as lumps of coal were to be tossed into coal cars serving industrial plants and seagoing vessels, eventually to find their way into furnaces—with disastrous results. The saboteurs were instructed also to destroy civilian morale by spreading incendiary devices in large department stores and by leaving time bombs in lockers at hotels, railway stations, and other places where crowds congregated.

So inattentive a student was Dasch that he had forgotten which chemical would bring out the message on the handkerchief—a problem the F.B.I. laboratory quickly solved. One of the addresses on it was that of a New York German whose house could be safely used by the saboteurs as a meeting place. Indeed, when the G-men got on the trail of Dasch's henchmen in New York, they discovered not only that the other four had already landed at Ponte Vedra on June 17 but that two of them —Kerling and Thiel—had also come to New York. What with the information obtained from Dasch and the handkerchief, it was a simple matter to arrest Burger, Quirin, Heinck, Kerling, and Thiel. That left only Haupt and Neubauer to be apprehended. Kerling was escorted by agents to Ponte Vedra, twenty-five miles southeast of Jacksonville, where he glumly pointed out the spot where he and his men had buried four German uniform caps and four boxes of explosives identical to those found at Amagansett.

The G-men worked in utter secrecy. Not a word had been given to the newspapers—a precaution that was continued, since publicity might hamper arrest of the remaining saboteurs. The case contained elements so ominous that Hoover kept his boss, Attorney General Francis Biddle, posted on it from the start. Biddle, in turn, reported to President Roosevelt, who was following developments with keenest interest.

Herbert Haupt, on leaving Florida, had gone to his home city of Chicago, with Hermann Neubauer following him in a later train. For the time being, young Haupt forgot about sabotage and devoted himself to movies, fun, and romance. Unknown to him, his skylarking was being watched by federal agents, who knew his home address and were waiting for him to lead them to Neubauer. When agents zeroed in on Neubauer at the Sheridan Plaza Hotel on June 27, both men were arrested.

Biddle telephoned the good news to President Roosevelt, who was determined that a speedy example be made of the eight in order to discourage further conspiracies. The President, in a memorandum to Biddle, gave his opinion that the two saboteurs who were American citizens were guilty of high treason, that the other six were in the category of spies, and that all deserved the death penalty.

This sort of punishment could be decreed only by a court-martial. In civil law, if one bought a gun with intent to shoot someone, it was not murder until the fatal shot was fired; and if someone arrived in the United States with heavy explosives but had not got around to using them, it was not sabotage. If the eight were tried in a civil court, they might get off with two or three years' imprisonment.

"I want one thing clearly understood, Francis," the President said. "I won't give them up . . . I won't hand them over to any United States marshal armed with a writ of habeas corpus."

Now at last it was safe to release the story—that is, part of the story. J. Edgar Hoover's statement to the press told briefly of the two landings, the buried explosives, the plan to cripple key industries and to kill and demoralize, and the eight men arrested. He did not say *how* they were apprehended. Nothing was said about the defections of Dasch and Burger, not only to prevent possible retaliation against them by their six comrades, or Nazi retaliation against their families in Germany, but also because there was no desire to enlighten the enemy about how the men had been caught. If Berlin believed that our counterespionage was superhuman,

Berlin might think twice before repeating such efforts.

The press and the public seized on the story as they would have embraced a great victory in battle. The *New York Times* gave it an unprecedented triple-banner headline and declared that the nocturnal landings from U-boats only a few hundred yards off our shores seemed like "a fantastic plot borrowed from the movies." The spectacle of the eight saboteurs sneaking across the Atlantic only to run into the arms of the waiting G-men contained perfect ingredients for national satisfaction. It made the Germans look comic and the F.B.I. heroic.

Not for days to come did the news leak out about the role played by Cullen and the Coast Guard at Amagansett. However, the actual facts of the capture still remained unknown. Cullen was promoted to coxswain (he later was awarded the Legion of Merit), while some observers urged that dogs be used to aid in beach patrols.

As for Georg Dasch, he was appalled to discover that instead of being hailed as a hero, he was a prisoner along with the seven others. He was in the familiar plight of the squealer, a man useful to the law but held in some contempt because his talebearing seemed dictated by expediency rather than idealism.

On July 2 President Roosevelt announced that the accused men would stand trial before a military commission composed of seven general officers—three major generals, three brigadiers, and the president, Major General Frank R. McCoy, Retired. The prosecution would be in the hands of Attorney General Biddle and the Army judge advocate general, Major General Myron Cramer. The defense was entrusted to Colonel Kenneth C. Royall and Colonel Cassius M. Dowell. More than a majority vote of the commission—five of the seven—was required for conviction and sentence. The rules of evidence would not be as restrictive as those protecting civilian rights. The President himself, as commander in chief, would make the final decision on the sentence on the basis of the commission's recommendation, and there would be no appeal.

Extraordinary efforts were made to keep the eight prisoners in good health until they faced the summary fate the public expected for them. They were placed in a second-floor wing of the old District of Columbia jail. Each man was kept in a tiled, ever-lighted cell with an empty cell on each side of him. He was clad only in pajamas, was allowed no writing materials, and ate his meals with fiber spoons off paper plates so that there was no opportunity for suicide. Only his counsel was permitted to visit him, and he could not communicate with the other accused men. He was guarded constantly by members of a detail of four officers and thirty soldiers. As Brigadier General Albert M. Cox, who as wartime provost marshal general of the District was custodian of

the prisoners, later put it, "Whenever a man requested a smoke, he was handed one cigarette. His guard lit the match. . . . Every instant for thirty-five days and nights, at least one pair of eyes was glued to each prisoner."

Reporters were excluded—an order that brought a howl from the press. Elmer Davis, the former newsman and radio commentator who had just been appointed director of the brand-new Office of War Information, had been promised full authority over censorship. He protested to Secretary of War Henry L. Stimson. Stimson, seventy-five and tart, let him know that the Army was in charge and that secrecy was vital. Davis next went to Roosevelt, urging that he allow censored accounts. The President relented only enough to permit a brief daily communiqué from General McCoy—a distinguished officer who would prove himself an execrable newspaperman.

Attorney General Biddle felt that the secrecy was overdone, that the public could have been informed far more completely without danger to the national interest, and that indeed virtually the only things that had to be concealed were the voluntary confessions of Dasch and Burger.

The most immediate menace to the Attorney General and his colleague General Cramer was a man named Milligan, who was long dead. In 1864 a Confederate sympathizer, Lambdin B. Milligan of Indiana, was arrested for pilfering munitions from Northern arsenals and sending them to the rebels. Denied a civil trial, he was speedily condemned to death by the military. However, President Lincoln was assassinated before he could sign the death warrant. Thereafter Milligan's attorneys fought the case through to the Supreme Court. The Court unanimously awarded Milligan a writ of habeas corpus. But five of the justices did more than that. Going well beyond the scope of the case at issue, they ruled that if a statute had permitted trial of a civilian by a military commission, the statute would have been unconstitutional. The military could not try a civilian as long as the civil courts were functioning. Only if actual invasion had driven out the courts could the military take over, and Indiana had not been invaded.

Biddle, knowing the caliber of the defense attorneys, was sure that they would exhume *Ex parte Milligan*. When they did, would the President of the United States and two of his cabinet officers be humiliated, and would sabotage be virtually sanctioned, and would the American public be outraged, by the removal of the case to the civil courts, where the eight men who had come to destroy would receive punishment of a kind given to purse snatchers?

The trial opened on July 8 in a long room on the fifth floor of the Justice Department building. The windows were swathed with blackout curtains. All of the defendants—who had confessed after their exhibitions of innocence and their fictitious identities had failed them—pleaded not guilty. The two turncoats, Dasch and Burger, testified that they had intended to betray the plot from the very beginning in Germany. Dasch, whom Mr. Biddle described to this writer* as "an interminable talker who made a poor witness," tended to irritate the judges, whereas the stalwart Burger made a better impression. He, after all, had good reason for his course. After the Gestapo's mistreatment of his wife and his own imprisonment and torture, he had vowed to betray Hitler (whom he had known personally) at the first opportunity. Even now he was worried that news of his collaboration with the prosecution might leak out and that his wife in Germany would suffer as a result.

As for the unlucky six, their bitterness against Dasch—and to a lesser extent against Burger—was quiet but evident. They were all caught in the same net. The law rewarded the quick squealer. They had not confessed as quickly as the other two and would be condemned for it. They were sure that no real effort would be made to defend them and indeed that their attorneys, Royall and Dowell, were actually spies for the prosecution. The two colonels had worked hard to win their trust, but they did not get it until they were able to arrange for the detested Dasch to be defended by another soldier-attorney, Colonel Carl M. Ristine. From then on the accused men came to understand more strongly with every succeeding day that they were being defended to the very limit of energy and resourcefulness by attorneys of superlative skill who knew all about *Ex parte Milligan*.

For each day's session the eight men were shaved by barbers, since a razor in their own hands might be used suicidally. They traded their pajamas for the clothing they had bought with Nazi money and were whisked by armored cars guarded with Tommy guns from their cells to the court over routes that changed with each trip. In the courtroom they sat diagonally across from the seven generals who would judge them—generals whose shoulders glittered with a total of twenty-two stars. Each of the unlucky six, though admitting he had arrived secretly by submarine from Germany with TNT and other explosives, gave the only argument open to him—that he had been trapped by fate or fear or military duty.

Young Haupt, pimply but dashing, swore that he had gone along with the plot only through fear of the Gestapo but that never in the world did he intend to carry out any sabotage. The curly-haired, solemn-faced Quirin said that he was actually afraid of explosives and would not have used them in this country or anywhere else. Heinck, the stolid machinist, pointed out that in Ger-

*Mr. Swanberg interviewed the former Attorney General at his home on Cape Cod shortly before his death in October, 1968.—Ed.

many it was dangerous to refuse such an assignment, but disclaimed any intention to put his training to use here. The balding Thiel said he thought Quentz Farm was a training center for propagandists and was appalled when he learned the truth. These four pictured themselves as deluded about Germany. They said they had seized upon the sabotage plan as the only means of getting back to an America they now appreciated and that they had arrived here somewhat in the nature of refugees from Nazidom.

Biddle left these arguments in shreds. He suggested that they might have received a welcome here instead of a trial had they only made all this known sooner. Instead they had followed every Nazi order, told no one about their doubts, moved stealthily about the country, registered at hotels under fictitious names, carried fraudulent papers, and lived comfortably on Nazi money until the moment of their arrest—after which they still tried to maintain the fiction until they saw it was impossible.

Only Kerling and Neubauer (although they also doubted that they could have carried the plot through) took the defense of a soldier's duty. The handsome, bushy-haired Kerling said that for him to have disobeyed orders would have been cowardly, while the burly Neubauer testified, "As a soldier you are not supposed to think; and I did not. I just got the order and I didn't know what for."

Colonel Royall knew that however necessary these assertions were, they would never save his clients' necks. His second line of defense was that even if the defendants could be shown to be guilty of clandestine conduct, that was the extent of their crime. They had not even attempted any spying or violence, much less achieved any. But the last line of defense was *Milligan*.

Had newsmen been present, they would have depicted the drama between the two men charged with most of the oral presentation, Francis Biddle for the prosecution and Kenneth Royall for the defense. Biddle, eight years the senior, was a tall six feet two, Royall a towering six-five. Each had studied law at Harvard, and each had sharpened his abilities under a titan of jurisprudence—Royall under Felix Frankfurter at college, Biddle as secretary to Associate Justice Oliver Wendell Holmes after graduation. Each had become an eminent attorney, Biddle in Philadelphia, Royall in his native North Carolina. Each in his lifetime would be a cabinet member, Royall slated to become the first secretary of the same army whose executioner's efforts he was now trying to thwart. And now each was serving the country in a wartime role that brought them into sharp, but always courteous, legal collision.

Royall made it clear at the start that he would challenge the legality of the President's proclamation and that all his arguments in the military court would not imply any concession that the military was competent to try the prisoners. This course brought an anguish of doubt to his defense colleague, Colonel Dowell. Unlike Royall, Dowell was a Regular Army man, with forty years of service behind him. He could not entirely quell a feeling that it would be insubordination for him to question a proclamation of his commander in chief. While he did not oppose the move, his uncertainty was so strong that he could not actively support it either, which left it up to Royall.

The Supreme Court was in summer adjournment, its members scattered. Royall cleared the way by applying to the district court for leave to file petitions of habeas corpus—a plea immediately refused. He talked with the Attorney General. The next day Royall and Biddle flew together to Chester Springs, Pennsylvania, where Associate Justice Owen J. Roberts was vacationing on his farm with Associate Justice Hugo L. Black as his guest. There, over country cheese and crackers, the two jurists listened at length to the callers. Roberts ended by telephoning Chief Justice Harlan Fiske Stone at Sugar Hill, New Hampshire, where he was spending the summer. The next day the nation learned that the Supreme Court would convene at all speed for the sake of men who were described by some commentators as "saboteurs, bomb-throwers, and killers." While a few of the justices were within reasonable distance, Justice James Byrnes was in South Carolina, Justice Frankfurter was in Connecticut, Justice Frank Murphy was an Army colonel training in North Carolina, and Justice William Douglas was in Oregon.

To a lawyer, appearing before the Court is equivalent to a pietist meeting the choir of angels. It is never easy, even for one like the Attorney General, who had done it repeatedly. The younger Royall had done so only once before. The two attorneys, though they had expert aid in research, got little sleep as they prepared their opposing presentations. This was the biggest spy case in American history. It was the first time the Court had broken its summer recess in twenty-two years. It would hardly do to present arguments not well founded in law.

Although there were many precedents involved (Biddle cited forty-eight, Royall sixteen), the Milligan ruling was at once the most striking and the one that seemed most promising for the defense. Royall portrayed the analogy to the Court, one of whose members was his old professor Frankfurter. No more so than Milligan's Indiana, he said, could the beaches of Long Island and Florida be called "zones of military operation." There was no combat there; there was not even a threatened invasion, much less an actual one. The civil courts were

functioning, Royall went on to argue, and they were the proper places to try the prisoners.

But the two days before the Court, the thousands of words spoken by the opposing counsel, and the many questions asked by the justices demonstrated among other things that Milligan was not the man he once had been. The Attorney General declared that the old case no longer applied—that time and technology had wiped out its relevance: "The United States and Nazi Germany are fighting a war to determine which of the two shall survive. This case is . . . part of the business of war." The swift total war of 1942 was as different from the static land warfare of 1864 as a Stuka bomber was from a musket. This war was everywhere—on land, in the water and air, and in our factories and civilian morale as well as on the battlefield. The saboteurs, arriving secretly in enemy submarines, had penetrated our defenses, bringing explosives. Like spies of all ages—like Major André and our own Nathan Hale—they had removed their uniforms and come in disguise. The universally accepted law of war was that spies should be tried by military tribunals and executed if guilty.

As for Chief Justice Stone, he was able to distinguish the case from *Milligan* because the saboteurs were belligerents from a foreign country. He was more troubled by the secrecy of the trial, and he wanted to show that the law of the land still governed. Yet the President had already been chided by this very hearing, and it was difficult to say that he had violated the Articles of War, which were not entirely clear and perhaps were never intended to bind him. On July 31 the Court, which tends to support the President in time of war, upheld the Attorney General unanimously.

Although the decision merely meant that the military trial would continue, it was the end of the line for the saboteurs. On August 3 the generals gave their verdict —death for all eight defendants—to President Roosevelt as the court of last resort. He followed Biddle's recommendation in commuting the sentences of Dasch to thirty years and of Burger to life imprisonment as rewards for their aid. It was the duty of General Cox, as provost marshal general, to inform the eight individually of their fate. The six condemned to die, he later reported, "seemed stunned and turned pale although they kept silent." The cool Burger, who was lying on his cot reading the *Saturday Evening Post* when Cox entered, looked up long enough to get the news of his life term, said, "Yes, sir," and returned to his reading. Dasch, whose disillusionment had been painful ever since his arrest, was outraged at his sentence. He wrote to President Roosevelt declining to accept the verdict—a dissent that was entirely rhetorical, for he was bundled off with Burger to the federal prison at Danbury, Connecticut.

Astonishingly, the doomed six signed a statement expressing appreciation for having been given a fair trial and adding, "Before all we want to state that defense counsel . . . has represented our case . . . unbiased, better than we could expect and probably risking the indignation of public opinion. We thank our defense counsel . . ."

The electric chair on the jail's third floor was readied for use. On August 8, in strictest secrecy, the six men, starting in alphabetical order with Haupt, were executed one by one. "Haupt was seated in the electric chair at one minute past noon," General Cox recorded. "The last of the six was pronounced dead at four minutes past one." It established a gruesome statistic—ten and one-half minutes per man, the swiftest multiple electrocution ever carried out.

The watchful press had learned of the electrical preparations, and reporters were standing outside in the rain. As *Time* put it:

In the courtyard, in the drizzle, six sheeted bodies on stretchers were loaded in ambulances . . . Steel-helmeted soldiers, with bayonets and machine guns, kept a little crowd of the curious away. The ambulances swung out slowly on the wet pavement, took the bodies to the Walter Reed Hospital for autopsy. . . . The U. S. still knew less about the case than about any one of its daily, tawdry crimes of passion.

In fact, not even the press knew until weeks later that the six men were buried in the District of Columbia Potter's Field at Blue Plains. The headstones consisted of unpainted boards bearing only the numbers from 276 to 281.

If it was true that newsmen and some libertarians were offended by the heavy cloak of secrecy, this policy did succeed in concealing for the war's duration the fact that Dasch and Burger had betrayed the plot to the F.B.I. This seemed to have one salutary effect: the Nazi *Abwehr* was stunned by the quick failure of its enterprise. At the time of the arrest of the eight, Colonel von Lahousen noted in his diary, "Since early morning we have been receiving [radio] reports . . . announcing the arrest of all participants in Operation Pastorius." The diary also disclosed that Hitler, in a rage at the debacle, gave the colonel and Admiral Canaris a tongue-lashing. So impressed were the Germans by the skill of the F.B.I. that they made only one further effort at sabotage in the United States during the war—a minor one that failed.

In 1948 Dasch and Burger were released from prison and deported to Germany. The garrulous Dasch had never stopped projecting a picture of himself as a loyal American who had risked death to foil a Nazi plot that otherwise would have cost untold numbers of lives and millions of dollars in war production—a man who, instead of being rewarded for valor, had been duped by the G-men, railroaded into prison, and then banished.

W. A. Swanberg has written highly acclaimed biographies of two American journalists, William Randolph Hearst and Joseph Pulitzer, and is now at work on a third, on the late Henry Luce of Time, Inc.

A major souce for this article was They Came to Kill, *by Eugene Rachlis (Random House, 1961). Three of the key participants in the affair later wrote their own accounts: Francis Biddle in* In Brief Authority *(Doubleday, 1962), Georg Johann Dasch in* Eight Spies Against America *(McBride, 1959), and former provost marshal Albert M. Cox in "The Saboteur Story" in the* Records of the Columbia Historical Society, *1961. In addition to consulting these and other pertinent books and articles, Mr. Swanberg corresponded with F.B.I. Director J. Edgar Hoover and interviewed both former coastguardsman Cullen and former Attorney General Biddle.*

Germany also became hostile toward him. German newspapers described him as a traitor who had saved his own skin by sending six comrades to the electric chair. Thereafter he was hounded from town to town, occasionally spat upon or threatened, unable to hold for long jobs as a waiter or bartender. Several times his life grew so uncomfortable that he took refuge in Switzerland. He kept writing plaintive letters to the American Civil Liberties Union, J. Edgar Hoover, Attorney General Tom Clark, and eventually to President Eisenhower, seeking permission to return to the United States. In 1959 he wrote a book published in this country, *Eight Spies Against America*, which he hoped would be sold to the movies and would justify what he described as his courageous anti-Nazi, pro-American adventure. One point he made was that he had voluntarily surrendered some eighty thousand dollars to the United States government instead of skipping off to the South Seas with it.

But one of the conditions of the suspension of Dasch's prison sentence and his deportation was that he would not be allowed to return. The ban was never lifted. Even the lost eighty thousand dollars seemed to gain him no sympathy. He could never win a particle of the esteem enjoyed by another man who had lost money— young coastguardsman Cullen. Cullen had turned in the $260 that Dasch gave him to his commanding officer. "I never thought to get a receipt for it," he recalls, "so it went to the government. I never really missed it."

The Sage of Topeka

By ISRAEL SHENKER

Landslide is not a word formed from Landon, the last name of the man who in 1936 was the Republican nominee for President of the United States. But it might just as well have been.

In the election of November 3, 1936, Alfred Mossman Landon got 16,681,913 votes—compared with 27,751,612 for winner Franklin D. Roosevelt. While Roosevelt swept 523 electoral votes, Landon won only eight—those of Maine and Vermont. Small wonder that Maine and Vermont were thenceforth looked on as states and cases apart—and that Landon became a synonym for landslide.

"The nation has spoken," Landon wired his victorious opponent. "Every American will accept the verdict and work for the common cause of the good of our country. That is the spirit of democracy. You have my sincere congratulations."

Today Landon tends his forty acres in Topeka and owns three Kansas radio stations: WREN in Topeka, KEDD in Dodge City, and KSCB in Liberal. He is still in the oil business, describing himself as "the smallest kind of operator." He has oil wells in eastern Kansas (he also has gas wells in the western part of the state); some are forty years old and average about a barrel or two a day. "In these little wells," he says, "the margin of profit is very small. Any change in taxes will probably mean the abandonment of some of the wells."

Landon and his wife, Theo, live alone in a vast white mansion that would serve a President nicely, and the passion of his life is what it has been these many years: politics. He celebrated his eighty-second birthday last September, but he still visibly delights in recalling the great days of his greatest national prominence.

If I had 1936 to do over again [he began] I shouldn't have been so conscious of the necessity to keep my record tied to the record of the Republican Party in the Congress. I shouldn't have leaned over backward to mention Republican harmony in every speech.

And when Roosevelt said it was the little acts that kept us out of war, I'd have pointed out that the breakdown of the London Economic Conference—which took place at the beginning of his administration—was one of the little acts that would get us into war.

I would have developed more arguments on foreign policy. I would have questioned more definitely and thoroughly than I did—more aggressively—his administration in handling the so-called welfare state.

It might have affected more electoral votes, but I don't think it would have been enough to elect me President. As soon as I was nominated for the Presidency, I sent for two bankers and asked what economic conditions would be from then until the election. They said each month would be better than the last.

Americans have a rough rule of thumb by which they judge the President—by how good or bad times are. So I knew right then I couldn't win.

I'm not making any excuses. I'm just saying that was the situation at the time.

He recalled the preconvention maneuvering.

I accepted an invitation to speak at the annual dinner of the Ohio State Chamber of Commerce in 1935. At breakfast the Ohio national committeemen told me it was all set up for Bob Taft to enter the convention as favorite son and would not take kindly to anyone who came in and tried to upset that.

So I told them they were going to be upset.

"You mean you're going to enter?" he asked, and I said No, but Borah's [Senator William E. Borah, Idaho Republican] certainly going to enter.

Then Borah did enter Ohio. Frank Knox [a Chicago newspaper publisher who was to become Landon's running mate] called me the next morning and said, "I'm leaving in an hour for Boston. If you don't enter Ohio, I will. I want you to call me in Boston and let me know."

I said, "All right." I didn't call.

He called Roy Roberts of the Kansas City *Star*, and wanted to know what I'd do. Roy said, "He's a stubborn Scotsman and insists he won't enter any favorite-son contests."

A political reporter for the Wolfe papers said Mr. Wolfe would underwrite my campaign, and I said that's one reason I'm not going to enter Ohio or any other state. I'm not going to be under obligations to any man.

There were two reasons I didn't contest any favorite-son elections. One was money. We limited contributions to twenty-five hundred dollars. Roy Roberts said he'd never seen so much money shaken under the nose of a candidate—and refused. The second reason was that I thought the election was a tough enough fight, and I wanted to preserve party harmony.

Now 82, Alfred M. Landon, Republican candidate for President in 1936, poses outside his Topeka home with his saddle horse, Red.

Landon discussed the Presidency of Herbert Hoover, and Hoover's role in Landon's own election campaign.

Mr. Hoover served a very useful life as an ex-President. The only thing he couldn't get over was his feeling that he should be nominated again, and that his administration should be defended.

Before Hoover became President, several reporters used to call on him regularly. He was Secretary of Commerce then, and there was no one from whom they could get such a clear description of problems and policies. When he became President, however, he just froze up. It's like the common case of junior executives who can outline a policy for their company that's perfect, but when they become chief executive they can't carry out the policy they advocated. That was Mr. Hoover.

To give him his due, I think it must be said that he saw 1930 coming. But he never did anything about it— or if he did it was too little and too late. When the banking crisis came in Detroit, Hoover threw in forty or sixty million dollars. If he'd thrown in forty million three weeks earlier, or if he'd thrown in one hundred million when he threw in forty or sixty, it would have done some good. I'm not objecting to what he did—but to what he didn't.

Hoover came here to see me for lunch one day during my campaign. He was sore because I wouldn't make a defense of his administration. When the newspapermen heard Hoover was here, they wanted him to come out to a dinner they had previously arranged and spend some time with them. Hoover agreed. That night Roosevelt was speaking at Pittsburgh. Most of the reporters were for Roosevelt, though most of them were my friends.

We were listening to Roosevelt's speech on the radio, and every time Roosevelt said "Hoover," the crowd booed. I was afraid to look at Hoover. Somebody told me afterward his face was frozen. Finally I said, "Mr. Hoover, I expect you'd better leave for the train." Of course we were way ahead of time.

Landon would like the record to show that he was not an isolationist, either in the campaign itself or afterward.

You'll find a page in my Indianapolis foreign policy speech in October '36 in which I said that the Neutrality Acts were the way to war. They'd make the aggressor think that the American people would not fight no matter what happens. And that was not true. Who was it who had signed the Neutrality Act? Mr. Roosevelt.

So then President Roosevelt called a special session of Congress to repeal the Neutrality Act. He started to use our destroyers. He expanded the Lend Lease Act far beyond the intent of the Congress. All this fuss over Johnson and the expansion of the Gulf of Tonkin Resolution —that was nothing compared with what Roosevelt did.

As I said in November '36, there wasn't anyone more isolationist in the country than Franklin Roosevelt. When he finally decided to ask Congress to repeal the Neutrality Act, he wanted me to back the move. I'd had a talk with Cordell Hull, and I called his attention to my Indianapolis speech. I said all the President can expect when he changes his position is silence from the opposition.

Roosevelt wasn't showing any leadership. I'd have supported him if he'd taken the leadership. But he wanted me to take the leadership and advocate repeal of the Neutrality Act. You don't mobilize support by saying, "Go over the top, boys!" You say, "Come on, boys, follow me!"

I can show you a speech I made in Chicago—in '39, I guess—in which I said it was to our interest, to America's interest, to challenge Hitler and Mussolini. Did Roosevelt support that? No. If he was waiting for support, there it was.

The record established by his opponent in the years after 1936 did not endear the President to Mr. Landon.

Roosevelt had plenty of time—he didn't need to sneak into a European war. I'd urged him repeatedly to go to the American people with his policy. I said in speeches that no one could be sure of what his policy was. Do we have to have a President sneak us into war?

When Frank Knox was offered a position in Roosevelt's cabinet [as Secretary of the Navy], Knox said he'd be in the position of a traitor if he didn't get me to be in the cabinet as well. But I was firm against the idea of going into the cabinet, since I wanted to preserve the validity of the two-party system. My own point of view was that we could have national unity in a much simpler and more acceptable way than by having me in the cabinet: all the President had to do was to take himself out of the third-term race.

The President deliberately put on an act when Frank Knox brought up the third term. He said, "Frank, I couldn't run again." And he held out his shaking hands to show the condition he was in.

If they hadn't passed that Constitutional amendment, I'd have been opposed to Eisenhower having a third term. Two things have been pretty plain in history. When you cut off circulation from the bottom to the top and assure the continuity of one person in office, you lay the foundations for the destruction of the republic.

In the declining years of the leader he always is weakened physically and mentally. One of the greatest crimes perpetrated in the country was Roosevelt campaigning in 1944 as a healthy man. He wasn't healthy, was he? Look at Yalta.

Truman himself said that President Roosevelt had become his own Secretary of State. You know, when a Secretary of State has had a formal conversation, he dictates a memo for the file. Roosevelt had all kinds of conversations with Stalin and Churchill and others, and all Truman could find were scraps of paper.

I said this country was in danger of becoming fascist if it re-elected Roosevelt in '36. Fascism, of course, was too strong a word. You didn't have the internment camps, the terrible brutality of fascism or communism. But the personal form of government that Roosevelt aimed at comes closer to being fascist than anything I can think of.

I don't question personal ambitions unless they infringe—as I think Roosevelt's did—on the principle of maintaining democratic processes. I wasn't vindictive about his victory. I knew he was going to win from right early, so there wasn't any disillusionment either.

"I never did lose my interest in foreign affairs," he says. When Harry S. Truman went to the support of the South Koreans in 1950, Landon in a speech at Colgate University supported the President. "At Colgate I said that Truman had probably acted unconstitutionally, but he wasn't the first President to do so. Theodore Roosevelt had acted unconstitutionally in Panama." In the fall of 1961, at the National Press Club, he spoke out in support of the European Common Market. The White House, which had advance notice of his speech, was delighted, he recalls. "I spoke on December 8, and President Kennedy on the sixth in New York, before the National Association of Manufacturers' national convention. If you care to go to the trouble, you'll find a great deal of similarity between my speech—a copy of which reached New York a couple of days before the President spoke—and the President's speech." And he has been urging the admission of Red China to the U.N. since 1948.

In addition to his interest in foreign affairs, Landon has also remained a keen observer of the political scene, and he talks freely—and independently—about the men, Democrats as well as Republicans, who have held the office he vainly sought in 1936.

Truman made a damn sight better President than I expected, just as Nixon is making a better President than I expected. There was no hint in Truman's record to match Roosevelt's, and I didn't see anything in Johnson's record that fitted Kennedy's—certainly not enough to be named Vice President on the ticket with Kennedy. In both cases it was a marriage of convenience.

Early in Truman's administration I said he'd probably go down in history as a great President. He didn't pull any punches. He laid things on the table family

SY SEIDMAN COLLECTION

Landon's campaign button had a sunflower, the state flower of Kansas, and showed him at 49.

style. He didn't wait for anyone to break the ice for him.

I don't think Truman used federal projects the way Johnson did to get senators' support—highways, dams, post offices. Johnson got his measures through by trading for them. Truman got his through by fighting for them.

I felt sorry for Dewey when Truman beat him. I sure thought Dewey was going to win in '48. I don't know anybody who didn't. And I had a lot of respect for Dewey, but it was his own fault—losing that '48 election. He didn't do anything to win it.

Dewey never had a sense of humor, and neither did Hoover. I remember telling Dewey, "Tom, it's better to lose big. If you get only Maine and Vermont you don't wake up in the middle of the night and think if you did this or did that, things would have been different." Dewey never cracked a smile.

Mr. Landon quickly turned his attention to the Republican who returned his party to the White House in the election of 1952.

I wasn't for Eisenhower because I didn't think a general has the training to be a President. He's been trained in just one thing: how much that hill over there's worth in terms of casualties to take or defend. After eight years of Eisenhower I saw no reason to change that view. Some people might say he was a do-nothing President, and I wouldn't argue with them.

After '64, Ray Bliss, who was chairman of the Republican Party, organized a meeting of Eisenhower, Dewey, and myself, plus the Republican leaders of the House and Senate. I didn't go, because I considered it an exercise in futility. But I sent a proposal on conflict of interest, a proposal that covers gifts to an ex-President as well as one in power, like valuable blooded cattle, like having his buildings remodelled free by firms that do business with the government, like accepting expensive equipment for his farm. My proposal even covered the case of people whose brothers are President, and senators and congressmen who continue in law firms representing big corporations.

I didn't have a choice in November '64. I voted for Goldwater with about as much enthusiasm as Jim Farley voting for Roosevelt for a third term.

When Johnson won, he tried to accomplish too much at one time. His social program, welfare state, Great Society—he tried to do it so fast that he didn't have the experienced men qualified to handle the new bureaus, and it got into the hands of politicians and graft.

And then came Vietnam. I said in '64, get in or get out. In October '64 Johnson was going to keep us out, and then, in February '65, came as complete a reversal as I've ever known a President to make.

I wasn't for Nixon's nomination in '60, but there was nothing I could do about it. As to Agnew, when '68 came, he was from Maryland and hadn't finished his second term. I didn't see anything in his record that really answered the question whether he would be qualified if called on to be President, and I didn't think it was a very good choice. I didn't think it strengthened the ticket.

I had a little feeling of sympathy and understanding for Humphrey. He was in something of the situation I was in in '36, when the Republicans were more interested in fighting Republicans than Democrats. Humphrey was tied so closely to the Johnson administration's policy on Vietnam that he couldn't fight it.

Once Nixon became President and announced his partial troop withdrawals, I thought it was a much more reasonable approach than [Clark] Clifford's—which didn't leave the Saigon government much time to adjust to it. How efficient the South Vietnamese army will be when we leave, only time will tell. I think maybe we ought to wait and give Nixon a little more time.

There is a legitimate argument that it makes a very basic difference what we do in Vietnam, and that all of Asia is concerned about what China would do if we pulled out.

I'll admit it's confusing. How can you expect a poor country boy to make a decision down here on the farm?

As far as the big picture's concerned, the Vietnam war is the number one issue, and all wars make emotional issues. But the basic issue is the continued debasement of our dollar. What have we accomplished except the loss of lives if we end the war and continue the debasement of our dollar?

Events at Chappaquiddick have persuaded Landon that President Nixon is likely to have a considerable period in office to work his will.

He's going to name practically all the Supreme Court and all the members of the regulatory agencies. So far he's appointing right-wing people and backing liberal policies.

I can remember old Civil War men who voted as they shot. It was Republican in the North, and Democratic in the South. Nixon's policy is not that sort—but his way is not unknown or new. If you ask me if his policy is wrong, I'd say it isn't an unknown policy, and we've survived the trading off of liberal policies against right-wing men.

Maybe today, with the growth of government in our social, economic, and political life, I'd have to say that the matter of appointments is more important than the matter of policies. In that gray area that exists in all regulatory areas—as well as in courts—the philosophy of the men becomes very important, more important than the policies.

I'm not saying Nixon's got it in the bag. Too many momentous events lie ahead. But he has the favorable position of the disorganized condition of a Democratic party that hasn't yet recovered from the convention.

I don't think we've got any new Nixon particularly. I think his campaign of '68 followed his campaign of '60. It's the times that changed. Nixon won it by keeping still—while college riots built up, and disorder, and chaos. He got by with the most general statements.

He developed into quite a politician. That's what the Democrats couldn't forgive. Look at the way he milked that [first] moon flight. He didn't have anything to do with the flight, but there he was getting the publicity.

Keeping current is what keeps Landon from feeling his age.

When you start worrying about your future, political or otherwise, you start growing old. I don't have time to think about the future, and it's never worried me. I figure on living like George Bernard Shaw, who said at ninety: "Oh, to be young again at seventy." I want to see what's going to happen. The whole world is at a turning point—the whole world is in chaos wherever you look: east, south, north, and west. But I don't think I'd be here if I'd won that election in 1936. The tensions and pressures would have been too much.

I've had the experience—thanks to losing—that comes to few men: of continuing to live my life afterward and be of public service in what some people, at least, call an objective mood, in a discussion of our public values and principles. In '36 some people said I was too objective to be a good candidate.

He does not regret his decision to return to Kansas after his defeat.

When I was defeated, Mrs. Landon said she'd be willing to do whatever I wanted to do, and there was talk of my running for the Senate. But what kind of education would our two young ones have had, dragging back and forth between Kansas and Washington? So we decided to stay here, and bought a hundred and sixty acres and built a house. We sold off enough land to pay for the house and pay for the ground, and leave us a nice little profit and forty acres.

We preferred the comparatively simple but more intelligent life of Kansas to Washington. There are some intelligent people in Washington. More of 'em in Kansas.

Israel Shenker, a reporter for the New York Times, *interviewed Mr. Landon recently in Topeka.*

THE BITTER STRUGGLE FOR A NATIONAL PARK

By JOHN G. MITCHELL

"We have permanently safeguarded an irreplaceable primitive area," said President Truman as he dedicated Everglades National Park in 1947. But what is permanence, and what is "safeguarded?" Did he speak too soon?

Even before there was an Everglades National Park, there was Clewiston. It is said to be the sweetest little city in America, having been sweetened by the United States Sugar Corporation, which raises cane and beef cattle there on 100,000 acres of flat Florida muckland. U.S. Sugar also owns the Clewiston Inn. In the southern comfort of the lounge, one can sit and admire the cane growers' tribute to the Everglades. It is a large, free-flowing oil canvas snugged around the windows and door and behind the polished bar, a romantic rendering of wild birds gliding above a wet landscape of cypress and saw grass, of alligators wallowing in the everglade sloughs. "How much did it cost?" a stranger asks, for the dollar is of eminent concern in Florida. The bartender says it cost $35,000, "and that was way back in 1935." He holds out a wine list. The prices of the liquor are on the front; on the back, keyed to the painting, the wild species are identified from left to right. "That's the way it used to be around here," says the bartender, gazing toward the window. "But it sure looks different now."

There was a time, once, when all of South Florida was like this painting. Great pearly thunderheads taller than mountains rolled off the Gulf Stream, and the rains slashed across the gray expanse of Lake Okeechobee, down the long curving river of saw grass—the true Everglades—into the mangrove swamps of the Shark River, Cape Sable, and Florida Bay. For one hundred miles, from Okeechobee to the tip of the Florida peninsula, the flat, sloping land, losing less than two inches of elevation to the mile, slowly carried the sweet water south over spongelike peats and limestone aquifers to mix finally in the brine of the Gulf. And with the flow of water came a flow of life duplicated nowhere on this planet. Great flocks of egret and ibis, by the hundreds of thousands, wings flashing in the tropical sun, whitened the sky as if to match the grandeur of the clouds themselves. In the mangroves and along the sloughs, white peli-

can and spoonbill and heron foraged the shallows for fish. And on the hammocks and in the cypress swamp and the drier pinelands, bear and panther and bobcat padded through the shadows, contributing their presence to the balance of Everglades life no less than the birds or the fish, the grass, the peat, the sun, or the rain. "When we try to pick out anything by itself," the naturalist John Muir once observed, "we find it hitched to everything else." Muir was describing what, in general, ecosystems are all about. It happens that his description profoundly reveals the secret—and, perhaps, the fate—of the Okeechobee-Everglades-Big Cypress region of South Florida.

In recognition of the region's unique natural values, the United States Congress in its wisdom authorized, at the lower end of this watershed, the creation of a national park, so that all of these biotic treasures might be observed in an environment far more appropriate than that of a Clewiston saloon. It was a fine idea. It still is. Yet before the park was created, the Everglades as an ecosystem had already been irrevocably altered. Today the thunderheads spill their waters across a landscape that has been drained, diked, and cultivated. The rich peats oxidize under the hot tropical sun. The Everglades grow bald, and the park receives most of its ancient overland flow not by the grace of God but through canals—and the goodness of the state of Florida and the U.S. Army Corps of Engineers. The water is no longer sweet. It carries chemicals from the farms and cattle ranches upstream. And some of these chemicals are contributing to the extermination of animal species in Everglades National Park.

Across the million and a half acres of citrus, melon, truck, and cane fields in central and southern Florida, DDT and other persistent chlorinated hydrocarbon compounds have been in heavy use. Milton Kolipinski and Aaron Higer of the U.S. Geological Survey in Miami sampled sediments from the Shark River Slough and from the Canal 67 extension,

the main pipeline into Everglades Park. They found that the sediments contain concentrations of chlorinated hydrocarbons in an order of magnitude one thousand times greater than that of the overlying water. Biological magnification through the food chain, a process in which each successive predator accumulates all the pesticide residues from the fats of its prey, often begins in so simple an organism as algae. Algae grow in the Canal 67 extension and the Shark River Slough.

On the desk of the superintendent of Everglades National Park, John Raftery, lies a copy of the U.S. Interior Department's list of this country's rare and endangered species. The fauna of the park are well represented: Florida panther, American crocodile, alligator, roseate spoonbill, wood stork. The southern bald eagle is also on the list. Kolipinski reports that bald eagle eggs in Everglades National Park are now showing DDT concentrations of twenty-four parts per million. Concentrations of twenty-six parts per million are already known to have so weakened the shells of falcon eggs that the weight of the nesting female crushed them.

By some accounts, then, Everglades National Park itself is being crushed in its 1.4-million-acre entirety and may soon be a terminal case. On the one hand, there is agriculture, pressing in from the north and east. On the other, along the coastal ridge between Miami and Palm Beach and in Collier County on the Gulf, urbanization and increasing population are placing new stresses on the region's resources.

With a population well in excess of six million, Florida now ranks ninth in the nation. Its net growth since 1950 has been an amazing 119 per cent. In fact, it is growing at a faster rate than California. Collier County has almost doubled its population in just nine years, and the combined population of Dade, Broward, and Palm Beach counties now approaches two million. The Florida Development Commission is delighted with these figures. In one brochure the

In the Big Cypress Swamp, which lies northwest of Everglades National Park and is part of the same ecological unit, a dragline digs up limestone to build a training strip for jumbo jets.

99

In March, 1969, Secretary of the Interior Hickel (pointing) and Florida's Governor Kirk (with pipe) visited the park to consider the plight of the alligator and to talk politics.

commission proudly points out that Florida's population density is 111 people per square mile, "as compared to 55 for the United States." And that, adds the commission, does not take into account the 600,000 out-of-staters vacationing in Florida on any given day. In one sense, the tourists are as essential to the economy of the Sunshine State as water is to the ecology of the park. "Come on down!" the ads for weekends in Miami once declared. Now bumper stickers try a new approach: "Help keep our state green—bring money."

What might well bring the most money (if not the "green") to South Florida is the Dade County Port Authority's plan to build an international jetport large enough to swallow the four biggest airports in America. The authority's favored thirty-nine-square-mile site in the Big Cypress Swamp was quietly purchased in 1968, and by last fall part of it had been turned into a training facility. Though the site lies at its nearest point a full six miles from the northern boundary of Everglades National Park, its development into a jetport would very likely have contaminated the water entering the park from the Big Cypress watershed. Forty per cent of the park's overland water is supplied by this watershed. The Dade plan has generated more notoriety, more conservationist ire, and more concern about environmental values than any single public works project

conceived in this nation, anywhere, at any time. As this article goes to the printer, the jetport in this site is dead, or mostly dead; but conservationists know that schemes so large, and so full of profit potential, often come back to life. Consider the size of it:

For openers, the Port Authority announced that its jetport would be served by a one-thousand-foot-wide "transportation corridor" paralleling the Tamiami Trail from Miami on the Atlantic Ocean to Naples on the Gulf. The corridor would encompass, it was hoped, a new U.S. interstate highway, a high-speed, air-cushion-ride transit system, and perhaps even another canal, a "recreational waterway" for hydrofoils and airboats. And finally, as the jetport grew, commercial and residential development would gather about the fringe of the site, generating all kinds of benefits to both Dade and Collier counties, the common boundary of which would be straddled by the jetport. By the year 2000, if one were to take the authority seriously, the site would have been ready to assume its manifest destiny as a spaceport for commercial rocket launching and recoveries, a sort of Cape Kennedy-by-the-Cypress.

"Alligators make nice shoes and pocketbooks"

Such schemes, not surprisingly, soon engaged the wrath of the nation's leading conservation organizations, and in particular the National Audubon Society, whose notable history in defense of the Everglades traces back to 1902, when the forerunner of the present society hired wardens to protect the egret rookeries from plume hunters. In a well known 1967 joust with the Army engineers, the society went to court to stop the corps from opening up Canal 111 and thus letting salt water into a vital fresh-water area of the park. It seems only proper, therefore, that the most dedicated and effective conservationist in the jetport fight has been the National Audubon Society's southeastern representative, Joseph Browder. And as the opposition flared, so did the tempers of the jetport's chief proponents. "Alligators make nice shoes and pocketbooks," said Michael O'Neil, Florida's Transportation Secretary, when asked by reporters about complaints that the jetport might destroy

the ecological balance of Everglades National Park. "I'm not really concerned about the alligators," O'Neil added. "And I don't miss seeing the dinosaur either." The director of the Port Authority, Alan C. Stewart, lumped all Everglades species together as "yellow-bellied sapsuckers" and went on to promise conservationists that he would build them an astrodome for butterfly chasing at the new jetport. His attacks on the opposition caused one wag to label him the "fastest lip in the East" and his superior to censure him for being "arrogant and offensive."

The approach of Stewart's top deputy, Richard H. Judy, was somewhat less heavy-handed. At one time an official for the Florida Highway Department, Judy waded into the fray evangelically, as if he were out to convert every last conservationist into a chamber of commerce booster. "This is going to be one of the great population centers of America," prophesied Judy. "Big Cypress Swamp is just typical South Florida real estate." At one point, Judy felt compelled to elevate his cause to Biblical heights. "We will do our best," he said in a letter to Dade County's mayor, Chuck Hall, "to meet our responsibilities and the responsibilities of all men to exercise dominion over the land, sea, and air above us as the higher order of man intends."

Judy's "higher order" was not necessarily everyman's, nor every politician's. When conservationists began to apply some pressure in Washington, the Secretary of the Interior, Walter J. Hickel, barely thawed from his gubernatorial reign in Alaska and still smarting from his confirmation-under-fire (no conservation for conservation's sake, he had said), flew to the Everglades to have a look for himself. Ostensibly the purpose of Hickel's visit was to publicize a crackdown on alligator poaching in the park, but behind the scenes he got an earful about the Dade-Collier jetport. What is more, Hickel discovered that Governor Claude R. Kirk, Jr., a fellow Republican, was perhaps less than enthusiastic about the Dade County Port Authority's favored site.

Hickel was good copy, almost as good as the rhetorical overkill being applied by the Port Authority. Concern for the Everglades began to spread well beyond Florida. In quick succession last summer

Life, *Look*, and *Business Week*, along with *Time* magazine's new "Environment" section, turned their editorial guns on the jetport. The *New York Times* dispatched the Pulitzer Prize reporter Homer Bigart to the scene of the contemplated crime, and the *Christian Science Monitor* sent its Pulitzer Prize winner, Robert Cahn. *Audubon* magazine led the pack with a stinging indictment of the jetport by Paul Brooks, author of *Roadless Area* and a past master of demonstrating that the pen is mightier than the slide rule.

Stewart and Judy of the Port Authority refused to give an inch. "We're going to prove once and for all," said Judy, "that public projects can be constructed to complement the environment and not destroy it." Before long, two prominent national agencies were putting Judy's claim to the test.

First out with its report, in September, was the Environmental Study Group of the National Academies of Sciences and Engineering. Though it stopped short of labelling the proposed jetport an ecological monster, the study group did raise some grave doubts—not about the welfare of alligators but about the good health of people. The report concluded that development of an international jetport at the Dade-Collier location would pose serious medical problems. "A few passengers each year," the academicians noted, "will be incubating malaria, dengue fever, filariasis. . . . The proposed jetport site is surrounded by a swamp that harbors many varieties of mosquitoes . . . it is possible that mosquitoes in the area could feed on an infected passenger and subsequently pass the disease to the Miccosukee Indians." But, the report added, if mosquito control were to be pursued with persistent pesticides (as it most surely would be), "this in itself may cause pollution problems . . . in Everglades National Park." And to that and similar notes, the academies' study group added another warning:

Unmodified ecosystems may become as important to ecology as a scientific discipline as primitive tribes have been to anthropology. The midwestern prairies in their original form have completely disappeared as have the virgin forests of the Northeast. The Everglades should not be allowed to go the way of these other environments, which were lost before they were scientifically understood.

Even as the academies' report was being circulated, the Interior Department released its own. This second study was to have been a co-operative venture with the Department of Transportation, home of the Federal Aviation Administration, which had contributed $663,000 to the jetport training field, but the final draft, hard-hitting and uncompromising in its opposition to the jetport, carried a disclaimer absolving the Transportation Department of any responsibility for the report's conclusions. It was not difficult for the outsider to understand why. Not only would full development of a commercial jetport and ancillary construction "inexorably destroy the South Florida ecosystem and thus the Everglades National Park," the Interior report charged, but the training airport itself is "intolerable . . . because the col-

lateral effects of its use will lead inexorably to urbanization and drainage."

Compiled by a team under the direction of Luna B. Leopold, senior hydrologist of the U.S. Geological Survey, the Interior report projected, at full development, a jetport that would service one million landings and take-offs a year and give rise to a residential-commercial community of 150,000 people. Such a jetport community would, according to the Leopold team, produce a few inevitable by-products: four million gallons of sewage and 1.5 million gallons of industrial wastes each day; ten thousand tons of jet-engine air pollutants scattered annually across the Big Cypress-Everglades watershed; disruption of the Miccosukee society, and extermination of at least one endangered species, the Cape Sable sparrow, through destruction of its habitat.

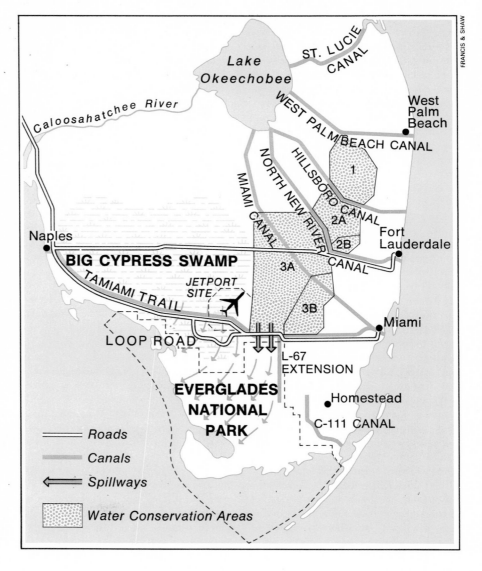

FRANCIS & SHAW

A pelican cannonball

There is also a grim warning in the Leopold report for the millions of air travellers who would use the Dade-Collier jetport. Bird strikes have been known to cause airplane crashes, and around the jetport site "flocks may exceed 50,000 and may include numbers of white pelicans and wood storks, species that habitually soar to high altitudes." The mature white pelican, incidentally, weighs about seventeen pounds. At more than 600 miles per hour any jet striking an object of that bulk would be striking a cannonball.

Finally, early this winter, a third study of the jetport and its environmental impact emerged. This one, commissioned by Dade County and executed by former U.S. Secretary of the Interior Stewart L. Udall's Overview Group, recommended construction of a "twenty-first-century" jetport at a new site in the Big Cypress, far enough removed from the park to minimize the impact on the wilderness of noise and pollution. Under the Udall plan, "people facilities" would be separated from "plane facilities." The terminal would be located in metropolitan Miami. There passengers would board a high-speed ground transportation system similar to the 200-miles-per-hour French Aerotrain, to be whisked directly to their waiting plane in the Big Cypress. The Udall plan would restrict jetport access to such a rail system; everyone using the port would therefore have to patronize the ground system. This, in turn, would generate sufficient revenue over the years to create a "conservation fund." If Udall has his way, the fund would repay bonds issued to finance public acquisition of the Big Cypress even before the jetport was completed. Udall thus would make development of the jetport contingent on the nondevelopment of the Big Cypress, and thereby assure protection of the park's vital western watershed.

The conservationists were clearly the victors of the Great Jetport Debate of 1969. They created a strong coalition that in September forced Governor Kirk and Secretary Hickel to agree not to support further construction of facilities at the Dade-Collier site. U.S. Transportation Secretary John A. Volpe—somewhat reluctantly, it would appear—went along with this. But there remained a major sore point between Hickel and Volpe: the training airport. Hickel was reportedly furious at Volpe's announcement of regulations governing the operation of the training field last November, when Hickel was away from Washington. He thought Secretary Volpe had agreed to consultation between their departments before taking action affecting the jetport. While pressure from environmentalists delayed operations at the training field, last fall its two-mile-long runway served as a magnet to new development in the Big Cypress. Some private landowners, in fact, petitioned for a new drainage district encompassing thirty-three thousand acres between the training field and the park. But with the agreement this January to allow Dade County to operate its training field with the firm understanding that a new site for the jetport will be found and the effects on the environment will be regularly monitored, development in the Big Cypress has been made a lot less enticing.

In the hearts of many environmentalists, there is a nagging fear that with the much-ballyhooed banning of the Everglades jetport they may have won nothing but time. Governors and Cabinet officers, crescendos of publicity and public outrage, come and go, but public works projects never die; they simply get shoved to a back burner, there to simmer until the next political turnover brings in a more appreciative chef. Meanwhile, for a great ecosystem and for Everglades National Park, other pots are brewing.

In Miami, James Redford of the Izaak Walton League wears a pained expression. His deep tan cannot hide it. "This kind of park is very, very hard to preserve," says Redford. For one thing, he points out, it is not the sort of national park that generates great public enthusiasm. Some 1.3 million visitors passed through Everglades' gates in 1968, but it is doubtful that a quarter of them were impressed by the scenery, as is nearly everyone who visits such parks as Yellowstone or Yosemite. Everglades is a biological park. Its drama is to be found in the spectacular display of wading birds, alligators, fish. For the trained observer it is a living laboratory in which one can see how things fit together in nature. But to the uneducated eye, most of the daily drama of plant and animal dynamics goes unnoticed. In consequence, the cheering section for Everglades National Park is skimpy.

In Florida, of course, everyone *says* he is for saving the park. Ranchers and cane growers are proud to have it down there, sopping up all that good second-hand fertilizer. They are proudest when there is plenty of water. When there is not (as during the 1962–65 drought), such sometime boosters of the park begin to regard it and its water needs in a different fashion. Suddenly the cry is "Alligators versus people!"—as if the park's values were somehow limited to the advancement of the reptile, and the interests of "people" were identical to those of the powerful agriculture interests.

The real issue, of course, is not animals versus people. It is a question of whether the state of Florida can continue to encourage unlimited residential and economic growth without precipitating ecological disaster not only to the park but to urban and agricultural interests as well. It is a question of the validity not of one park but of the entire national park concept, which holds that unique natural systems should be preserved intact for future generations as part of the nation's heritage. And finally, it is a challenge to all Americans, who have only recently awakened to the fact that modern man must learn to manage the environment he has so rudely manipulated. Ignorance, as it has been displayed in the case of the Everglades, is no longer a valid excuse. "This park," says Superintendent John Raftery, "could become the early warning system for America's total environment. If we can find an answer for the Everglades, a true solution, then we can find an answer for almost anything."

Promises of an "empire of the Everglades"

The Everglades have never yielded answers easily, except, perhaps, to the old Calusa Indians, who were there even before the first white sails appeared on the eastern sea. To the Cabots, Ponce de León, and de Soto, the New World of South Florida ended within earshot of the beach. Scouts venturing farther inland brought back reports of tangled hammocks and of a landlocked sea of strange, cutting sedge that slashed the flesh. This was no country for the gran-

The Tamiami Trail runs along a levee across the saw-grass river, and the flow of water to the national park (which is on the left in the picture above) is controlled by four state-operated water gates such as the one in the foreground.

dees of Spain, and for three hundred years Western man left it virtually untouched, a void on his maps.

Then a new breed, calling themselves Americans and hardened to discomfort on the Georgia frontier, came to the Everglades. They had been fighting Creek Indians in the northern swamps, and now they followed Andrew Jackson to Florida to evict the Seminoles, as they mistakenly called all the Indians they encountered there. For seven years the sound of war drums rolled across the Everglades. When they fell silent in 1842, the balance sheet showed four thousand Indians and runaway Negro slaves shipped off to Arkansas, fifteen hundred American men-at-arms and no

one knows how many Indians dead in the swamps. Many live Indians remained—and their descendants still do.

With statehood in 1845, Florida looked again toward the Everglades, this time for the land it would need to attract new settlers. In her history, *The Everglades: River of Grass*, Marjory Stoneman Douglas describes the fever of that turning point:

Many veterans of the Indian wars remembered now with pleasure the sea about those southern beaches and the sun glinting along the great levels of the saw grass, the unending openness, the great light, the fine air. They knew well the blackness of the sawgrass muck. The idea sprang up spontaneously that the Everglades ought to be drained. It was an idea more explosive than dynamite, and would change this lower Florida world as nothing had changed it since the melting of the glacial ice . . .

In 1882 Hamilton Disston, a Philadelphia entrepreneur, lighted the fuse. He moved his first dredge out of Fort Myers up the lower Caloosahatchee River, and the drainage began. He was soon followed by other enterprising gentlemen, including one Napoleon Bonaparte Broward, who ran for the governorship of Florida on the promise that "the Empire of the Everglades" could be drained for a dollar an acre. Broward reasoned that all one had to do was "knock a hole in a wall of coral" and let the water seek the level of the sea.

It was not quite that simple, for the "empire" of the Everglades is actually a vast basin that begins not at Okeechobee but one hundred miles north of the lake in the headwaters of the Kissimmee River near Orlando. Rainfall over this nine-thousand-square-mile area averages from fifty to sixty inches a year. Clearly, a hole in the coral would not suffice. So the dredges again proceeded upstream— up the Miami and New rivers; up the St. Lucie; joining Belle Glade to Boca Raton with the Hillsboro Canal—and all these sweetened the ocean with their runoffs.

In 1926 and again in 1928 hurricanes swept up from the Caribbean and sent the waters of that great shallow saucer, Lake Okeechobee, howling down across the cultivated fields and into the towns and cities clustered around the edge of the lake. More than two thousand people drowned in the floods. Those disasters brought a new "improvement" to the

Everglades: an immense levee, high enough that Okeechobee could never again overflow its banks as it had in those two dreadful autumns. And when the levee was completed, drought brought fire to the drained land below the lake. Even in Miami, the skies turned gray with smoke. "What had been a river of grass," wrote Miss Douglas, "was made in one chaotic gesture of greed and ignorance and folly, a river of fire." As far as some old-timers were concerned, the Everglades were finished.

Yet they were no more finished than the floods or the fires. Two hurricanes smashed across Florida in the fall of 1947, after a prolonged period of heavy rainfall, and left the farmers and townspeople holding a bill for $60,000,000 in damages. That settled it. In Tallahassee and in Washington legislators demanded action: increase the carrying capacity of the canals; have the Army engineers raise even higher the Okeechobee levee; and create water-storage areas to hold back the flood waters from the defenseless cities of Fort Lauderdale and Miami until the waters can be made useful to man —to irrigate his farmland and wet the limestone acquifers that keep sweet the drinking water of his cities. What Florida demanded, Florida got. They called it the Central and Southern Florida Flood Control Project. Over the next twenty years, the federal government was to underwrite this ambitious public works program to the extent of some $170,000,-000 (and that only half the project). But in 1948, so soon after the last great flood, Florida was satisfied just to get the project authorized. Ranchers and city slickers were so excited about the prospects that hardly anyone took notice of South Florida's other major event several months earlier—the official opening of Everglades National Park.

From the beginning, administrators of both the park and the Flood Control District (F.C.D.) have approached the critical problem of Everglades water like jealous twins tugging at opposite ends of a security blanket. Indeed, before either was a year old, a conflict was inevitable. Here was the flood control project seeking to harness the Everglades' historic flow; there was the park, whose entire biota depended on water—and plenty of it. "The question," Assistant Secretary of the Interior William E.

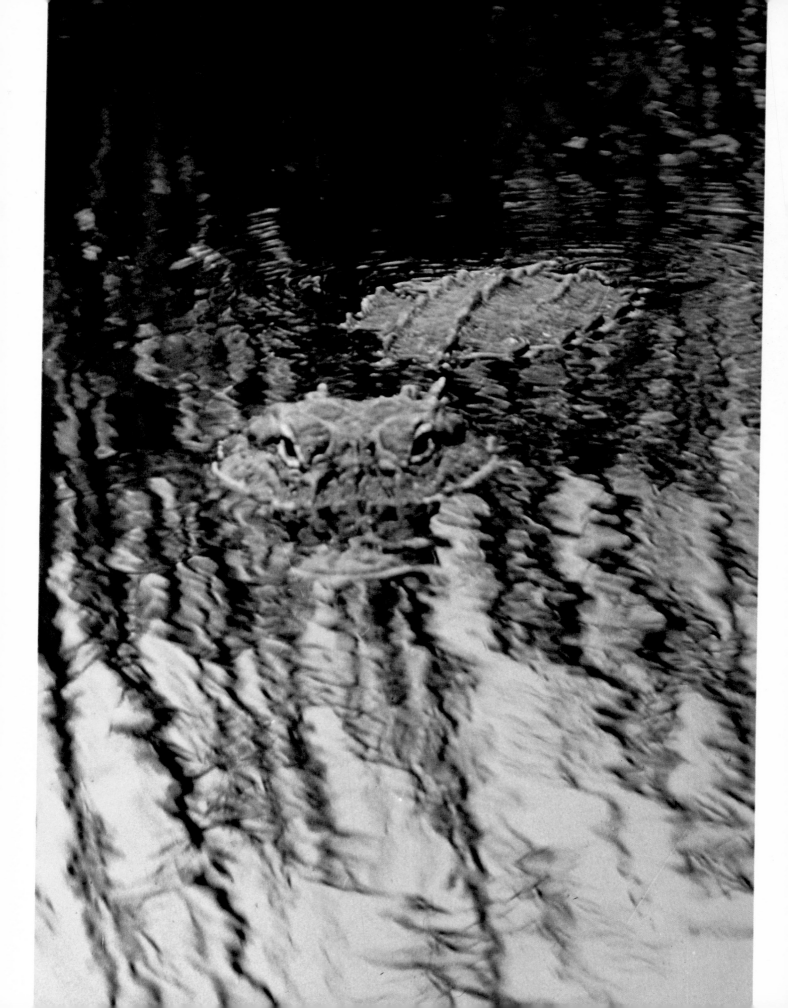

Warne declared in a letter to the Army's chief of engineers, "is not one of too much water, but a guarantee that there shall not be too little."

The record, of course, shows that far too little water to sustain a fragile ecosystem dribbled into the national park during the 1962–65 drought. In fact, 1962 marked the completion of Levee 29 along the park's northern boundary and the closing of floodgates along the Tamiami Trail. "Henceforth, flow would be artificially controlled," notes the Leopold report. "The River of Grass, after 5,000 years, had ceased to flow." In the park, water levels fell to an unprecedented low (at least in the annals of human mismanagement). Many species of aquatic life managed to survive in the park only because pockets of water remained in the deepest alligator holes and crayfish burrows in marl and limestone under the powder-dry muck. Dr. Frank C. Craighead, a well-known consulting biologist to the park, writing in 1968 of the alligator's "keystone" position in the ecology of the Everglades and of the incredible destruction of wildlife in the park during those drought years of the early 1960's, observed that "it seems reasonable to believe that [the alligators] now living represent a reduction to about one or two per cent of those present" before the man-induced droughts.

The park's riparian competitors argue that the old overland flow through the saw grass was insignificant even before the region was crisscrossed with dikes and canals. True, most of the park's water does come direct from the clouds: as much as 80 per cent of the total supply is the rain that falls on the park itself. Yet the remaining 20 per cent that would otherwise come slowly overland is essential, particularly after the rains have ended in October. "What flows in from the north," says James H. Hartwell, a hydrologist of the U.S. Geological Survey in Miami, "is the national park's lifeblood."

Based on a twenty-year flow pattern, hydrologists have determined that, in addition to direct rainfall, the park needs a minimum of 315,000 acre-feet per year (an acre-foot is the volume of water that will cover an area of one acre to a depth of one foot) flowing into the Shark and Taylor sloughs through the F.C.D.'s floodgates and canals. Another 157,000

acre-feet flow naturally into the park's western portion from the Big Cypress. Harking back to Assistant Secretary Warne's first appeal to the Corps of Engineers, which has operational jurisdiction over F.C.D.'s waterworks, the National Park Service is again attempting to obtain from the corps and the state of Florida a binding guarantee that it will receive its minimum requirement of 315,000 acre-feet.

"It's like asking someone to share cancer"

For its part, the F.C.D. insists that the corps has jurisdiction only over the floodgates and canals that supply the water, not the distribution of the water itself. Moreover, the F.C.D. so far has declined to guarantee any specific supply to the park. In times of drought, it argues, the park must "share in adversity." Some park officials wince at the very phrase. "Who ever thought *that* up?" one of them asks. "It's like asking someone to share cancer." Manuel Morris, the Park Service's chief troubleshooter in Everglades matters, is more flexible. "Sure," he says, "we'll share adversity —with the present water users. The trouble is, Florida keeps growing."

Lately, under the administration of Governor Kirk, the F.C.D. has assumed a more co-operative attitude toward the park. The old alligators-be-damned crowd has been retired from the district's board of commissioners. The present vice chairman (and former chairman), for example, is Robert Padrick, an amiable Fort Pierce auto dealer, a member in good standing of the Sierra Club, and Florida's "Outstanding Conservationist" of 1969. Padrick and F.C.D. Chairman Robert P. Blakeley are in a tough spot. Their three water conservation areas in Palm Beach, Broward, and Dade counties are almost as large as the park itself. In and from them, the F.C.D. must try simultaneously to meet the needs of agriculture, prevent flooding, recharge the Biscayne aquifer from which the coastal cities draw their potable water, and accommodate the park. Beyond those responsibilities is yet another: the conservation areas are perhaps South Florida's most popular and productive hunting and fishing grounds. Florida's Game and Fresh Water Fish

Commission estimates that the three areas generate up to $10,000,000 a year in recreation spending. "I feel as strongly about our conservation areas," says Padrick, "as Mr. Hartzog [George Hartzog, director of the National Park Service] feels about his park. It's not a question of which is better, ham or eggs. The two go together."

But not everyone is sure exactly *how* the two go together. Defenders of the park fear the power of the rod-and-gun lobby in Tallahassee (which fought successfully to delete 650,000 acres from the park's authorized area during a 1958 boundary settlement). They are afraid, for example, that the F.C.D. will regulate water levels in its conservation areas to accommodate the demands of hunters and fishermen.

Joe Browder, of the Audubon Society, is appalled by what the hunters' half-tracks and swamp buggies have done to the fragile saw-grass Everglades in the conservation areas. "The state is turning Florida into a zoo," complains Browder. "They'd stock the Everglades with giraffe if they thought they could sell licenses to shoot them. And they probably could."

At the moment the state is too busy with its new water resources plan. Written largely by the Corps of Engineers at the request of Congress, and supported by the Park Service as a partial solution to its problems, the plan calls for a variety of new water-control structures, including another vertical addition to Okeechobee's levee, so that the storage level of the lake can be raised four feet more than previously authorized.

As the new water plan moves ahead, scientists in South Florida are seeking answers to a variety of interlocking questions—questions about run-off and evapotranspiration, about oxidation and changes in plant communities—questions the public works engineers never learned how to ask until it was too late, or until they were dragged kicking to the query by the public discovery that somehow a healthy ecosystem might just happen to be as important as a healthy economy.

Among the unanswered questions, perhaps the most critical is this: Where does all the water in South Florida *go*? One place it goes is the ocean. Even in Collier County, now outside the

For thousands of years the alligator has been kingpin in the Everglades ecosystem. But his numbers have been so reduced by land drainage and hide hunters that he is threatened with extinction.

Roseate spoonbill in flight

Wild turkey

Reddish egret

Young bald eagles on the nest

Wood storks in silhouette (above); an anhinga dries his feathers (left).

Eighty species of birds nest in the park, and each one has its special habitat needs. The anhinga likes canals and sloughs; the wild turkey sticks to pine forests; the egret, spoonbill, and eagle nest in mangroves and feed in the bays; wood storks (also called wood ibis) prefer brackish or fresh-water marshes.

F.C.D.'s realm, new canals dredged by the Gulf-American Land Corporation and other speculative developers are pouring billions of gallons into the Gulf. But no one apparently knows how much. The loss from the east side of the Everglades is so great that the F.C.D. and the corps have included in their water plan provisions for an elaborate system of backpumping water, intercepting it before it reaches the sea and sending it back into Okeechobee and the conservation areas. Vice Chairman Padrick is excited about the backpumping scheme. But neither he nor the sharpest minds in the U.S. Interior Department can predict what effect the backpumped water might have on the lake and conservation areas, charged, as the water most certain will be, with all kinds of agricultural wastes and chemicals picked up in transit along the canals.

What often happens is *eutrophication*, the process by which a body of water dies prematurely from lack of dissolved oxygen, choked by a fatal bloom of algae. It is happening all over, and Lake Erie has long been the national prototype. Now scientists are beginning to look at 742-square-mile Okeechobee, the second largest lake wholly within the United States, for signs of the same fatal illness. And they are there. Not far from the inlet of Nubbin Slough, in the northeast corner of the lake, mats of algae grow green and thick in the still water.

"Even without backpumping," says Frank Nix, a Park Service hydrologist, "there's already so much fertilizer flowing down from the north that one of these days the entire lake could turn upside down." The nitrate and phosphate fertilizer stimulates the growth of plant life in the lake. And as old plants die and decay, they rob the water of its oxygen. Then the fish die. Estimates are that Lake Okeechobee is capable of producing fifty million pounds of edible protein annually—channel catfish and bream, mainly, and fish-eating ducks. If the lake should die, so will the fish and the wildlife. And so, at the other end of the pipeline, will the park.

The greatest loss of water in South Florida is caused by evapotranspiration. What comes down must go up, either directly from the heat of the sun or through the cells of green plants. The loss from the lakes of the Kissimee Basin, from

Okeechobee and the three conservation districts alone, is estimated to be the equivalent of seven million acre-feet a year. "Why, you wouldn't believe it," says Charles M. Wiesenfeld, the corps area engineer at Clewiston. "On a good hot day evaporation takes a quarter inch off the top of Okeechobee." With a little figuring, Wiesenfeld estimates that a quarter-inch across the whole, vast face of the lake amounts to 1.5 billion gallons—almost half as much water as the F.C.D. was sending each day into Everglades National Park last June, one of the wettest months in one of the wettest years on record.

"They're not farming that soil, they're mining it"

Faced with such prodigious losses, the corps and the F.C.D. are now investigating the feasibility of suppressing evaporation with monomolecular, paraffin-like films sprayed across the surface of the water. If even a 10 per cent reduction in evaporative losses could be achieved by such suppressants in Conservation Area 3, the volume of water saved would be more than sufficient to meet the national park's annual requirement of 315,000 acre-feet. Still, suppressants, like backpumps, could create ecological problems. Preliminary research with some compounds indicates that the monolayers inhibit the emergence of mosquito larvae, which represent a key link in any aquatic food chain.

As the water goes, so goes the peat-rich soil of South Florida. That is yet another loss, and it is an irrevocable one. In the days of Hamilton Disston, before the beginning of drainage on a massive scale, the Everglades muck lay fourteen to seventeen feet deep around the south end of Lake Okeechobee, tapering to shallower depths as the land sloped south. Then the canals carried off the water, and the muck was vulnerable —to fire, to wind erosion, to compaction, but most of all to oxidation, a kind of solid-state equivalent of evaporation. In some areas today, up to 40 per cent of the original organic soils is gone. In others, limestone outcrops rise in testament to the farmer's folly. Even under the best management, which dictates that fields not in production be flooded, the muck is oxidizing at the rate of nearly

an inch a year. "They're not farming that soil," says Browder of National Audubon. "They're mining it."

Physiographic changes no less dramatic are occurring within the park itself and are most visible not in the slope or thickness of soils but in the chameleon character of the park's plant communities. Aerial photographs taken of the lower Shark River Slough in 1940 and again in 1964, and analyzed by Kolipinski and Higer of the U.S. Geological Survey, show a decrease in wet prairie and saw-grass marsh habitat and an increase in shrub communities. Kolipinski and Higer report two likely causes for this change: shorter periods of inundation and loss of soil through oxidation. These same two forces may also be triggering massive ecological disturbances in the Big Cypress Swamp abutting the park. According to Joel Kuperberg, executive director of the Collier County Conservancy, a significant number of young, shallow-rooted cypress are dying from lack of water. Kuperberg blames the drainage. "The way it's going," he says, "we'll soon have a desert."

But even Kuperberg, as disheartened as he may be, doubts that a Sahara is *inevitable* in South Florida. There may yet be time to pull the loose ends together, to answer the questions men are only now learning to ask. There may even be time enough to save Everglades National Park, if the men who could make the right decisions are willing to make them.

The record of the park is replete with bad decisions—and no decisions. The first mistake was by an inept U.S. Congress, which permitted more than half a million acres already authorized for the national park to be excluded when boundaries were fixed in 1958. Now it turns out that the park's ecology has been disturbed by the development of these excluded areas. The National Park Service itself has been less than astute on a number of occasions. Biological research and management practices that should have been initiated a decade ago have only recently been implemented. Even worse, the Park Service has been slow to cope with immediate threats. In the case of the Everglades jetport, one park official actually gave his blessing to the Dade-Collier site because it was preferable to another site closer to the park.

The species thriving best in Florida congregates in ever swelling hordes. Some 600,000 a day now migrate there for brief stays with the 6,000,000 for whom it is an all-year habitat.

And when the full implications of the Dade-Collier site became known, it was not the Park Service that stirred up the conservationists. It was Robert Padrick, then chairman of the Flood Control District.

To be sure, a certain political realism pervades the Park Service's executive echelon. Money for new national parks is scarce enough, but money to expand or protect old ones is even dearer. Thus at least three different drafts of the long-awaited Everglades National Park "master plan" have been pigeonholed somewhere in the Interior Department; all reportedly urged—perhaps too emphatically—the acquisition of more land to protect the park's ecosystem.

Most observers whose job security is not wedded to Park Service policies agree that the preservation of the park is dependent on large-scale land acquisition, both of private inholdings within the park and of lands outside to buffer the park's vulnerable perimeter. The inholdings situation is critical. Inside the boundaries of the park some 3,500 individuals and corporations hold 74,000 acres. One area has been subdivided by a British syndicate that is selling the lots—sight unseen—to buyers throughout Northern Europe. In the so-called Lostman Five area, half a dozen new private fishing camps were completed last year. And in the 24,000-acre "Hole in the Donut"—where inholdings are protected from condemnation so long as they remain in agricultural use—pesticides from truck farms are pouring down the Taylor Slough into the park's principal habitat for bald eagles. To acquire these inholdings at today's land prices would cost the United States approximately $20,000,000.

Far larger appropriations would be necessary for the national government to acquire—as it should—those lands outside the park's boundaries which are believed to be the most essential for assuring continued flow of water into the park from the Big Cypress. One tract runs west from the vicinity of the jetport site and includes the Fahkahatchee Strand, a wild Collier County slough noted for its hanging orchids, strangler figs, moss-draped cypress, and royal palms. The Fahkahatchee, in fact, is being considered for designation as a national monument. Now some conservationists are promoting its hunting and fishing values as reasons to acquire it as a national recreation area. The second critical buffer lies in Monroe County south of the Tamiami Trail, in the Loop Road area between the park's panhandle and its northwest extension. Much of the land around here is high and dry enough to be vulnerable to development, and the rest of it feeds water directly into Everglades National Park.

At the very least, these lands in Monroe and Collier counties should be placed within a water conservation district somewhat similar to those managed on the east side of the Florida peninsula by the F.C.D. Creation of such a district was recommended by the Environmental Study Group of the National Academies as a measure to prevent the intrusion of salt water into the shallow aquifer underlying the Big Cypress Swamp, to assure an uninterrupted flow of surface waters into the western portion of the park, and to maintain an adequate water supply for the growing needs of southwest coastal communities.

Along with such solutions for the Big Cypress there must also come the guarantee that the national park will receive a minimum 315,000-acre-foot flow of water through the floodgates and canals of the F.C.D. Even those who are not enthralled by the challenge of maintaining the park's biotic integrity must surely be interested in maintaining the productivity of the multi-million-dollar commercial fisheries in Florida Bay and in the Gulf. The famed Tortugas shrimp, for example, grows to maturity in the mangrove estuaries of the park. Here the low salinity of brackish waters—controlled by the input of fresh water from the park's sloughs—protects the juvenile shrimp from predation. Durbin Tabb, a marine biologist of the University of Miami, warned more than five years ago: "If the park were to lose all of its supplemental water from the traditional watersheds . . . there is grave danger that the richest commercial fishery of the state would be seriously damaged."

In many respects there is a test case here for all Americans. In the Everglades are all the environmental stresses one is likely to encounter anywhere in the nation. It is no neat little package, to be sure, and as long as the jetport fight appears to have been resolved, public concern over the future of the Everglades will doubtless dwindle. But the park does reflect, in microcosm, the challenge that all citizens face wherever the landscape is being poisoned and the forces of nature abused. Indeed, if Everglades National Park is to be saved, it will be done because the discrete segments of our society will have found a way to work together. If that can be accomplished, then perhaps what the park has taught us can begin to save America.

John G. Mitchell is editor in chief of the Sierra Club and a former science editor for Newsweek *magazine. Patricia Caulfield, whose photographs of birds and animals illustrate Mr. Mitchell's article, will see the fruition of seven years' work with the publication next fall by the Sierra Club of her book,* The Everglades.

Now seldom sighted and his survival uncertain, the Florida panther finds his only shelter in the mangrove forests of Everglades National Park and the watery vastness of the Big Cypress Swamp.

More than a mile long, the huge Amoskeag textile mills (above) formed an unbroken wall along the east bank of the Merrimack River. The man responsible for the over-all plan of the complex was Ezekiel Straw, a talented civil engineer who later became president of the company and then governor of New Hampshire. In the photograph at left, taken by Lewis Hine in 1909, workers head home over one of the bridges that crossed the canal (below) to their company housing nearby. Highly progressive in its policies, Amoskeag offered employees medical care, playgrounds, language classes, and the chance to buy stock.

Epitaph for an American Landmark

In the year 1807 in the town of Derryfield, New Hampshire, a gentleman by the name of Samuel Blodget proclaimed: "For as the country increases in population, we must have manufactories, and here at my canal will be a manufacturing town—*the Manchester of America!*" Blodget (right) built his canal around the Amoskeag Falls on the Merrimack River, and in 1810 Derryfield (population: 615) indeed took Manchester as its new name. But the Amoskeag Cotton and Woolen Manufactory that evolved there would doubtless have amazed even the prophetic Mr. Blodget. Construction of new mills began in 1831, backed by Boston money. Two years later President Andrew Jackson paid a visit and was much impressed by "all these spindles in motion." By 1845 Manchester had a population of ten thousand, and forty years after that the Amoskeag complex was the biggest concentration of textile mills in the country, if not the world. No other place could match it. By 1915 the mills were employing fifteen thousand people and were turning out cloth at an incredible fifty miles per hour.

But apart from its colossal scale and its very considerable importance to the new industrial America then emerging, the Amoskeag complex was a unique and highly successful product of total planning. Unlike virtually every other industrial community in the country, the whole affair had been worked out on paper in advance, and with remarkable foresight and common sense. Except for a few Victorian towers and gateways, the buildings were quite plain and simple. But it was the arrangement of everything, the cobblestone streets with their white granite curbstones, the neat red brick houses for the workers, the mills, warehouses, and bridges, that gave the place its special appeal. "The handsomest manufacturing city in the world," it was called, and rightfully so. Like its immediate predecessor, Lowell, Massachusetts, Manchester was founded on the early nineteenth-century utopian idea of providing for the complete life of the new industrial man, all within a carefully organized community. (In Manchester, U. S. of A., there would be none of the squalor of Manchester, England!) The town was treated as an architectural unity, built on the gentle curve of two

The History of Manchester, BY C. E. POTTER, 1856

In the name of progress one of New England's most historic and unusual urban areas is being carved into parking lots

parallel granite-lined canals more than a mile in length, which served as the principal power source for the mills. To get to the mills in the morning "the enterprising citizens" had only to cross the canals directly opposite their houses, passing over bridges and through archways in much the same way as in a medieval cathedral close, while trains and trucks were able to run unrestricted the full length of the yard between the mill buildings, out of sight and hearing from where people lived. The plan struck a balance between the needs of industry and the needs of people, and that was rare in urban America, then and since.

But starting about fifty years ago, like countless other New England textile towns, Manchester fell on hard times, and in another generation the old mills on the river were looked upon by most townsmen as scarcely more than huge symbols of economic gloom.

As a result the great Amoskeag complex has become another tragic victim of twentieth-century urban "renewal" and of a typical shortsighted caving in to the demands of the automobile. Economic vitality has returned to Manchester through other kinds of manufacturing, but to judge by what the city has done with its historic old mills, a new kind of bankruptcy of spirit and imagination appears to have set in. Instead of making an all-out effort to produce a plan befitting a vital and confident community, urban renewal has carried out only the most obvious stopgap measures, wiping out whole city blocks for parking lots.

Demolition began last year, along lines established a decade ago in a report drawn up by Arthur D. Little, Inc., a Massachusetts-based consulting firm. So far nearly all the long, curved buildings bordering the canal and two large mills have been torn down. Part of the great wall of brick buildings along the river will also be destroyed. Once the demolition is complete, the canals will be filled in. Not a single building is to be built on the urban renewal site except for an industrial sewage plant that will replace two blocks of the original housing (still in use) and thus ruin the essential continuity of what architectural historians have called New England's handsomest cluster of nineteenth-century company houses. Two roads, sixty

A 1969 aerial view of the Amoskeag, a "new town" of its day, shows the Merrimack (upper left), the main mills bordering the river, the long mill yard (note the same tower as on page 110), the "canal buildings" that screened off the yard from where the workers lived, and the moatlike canals with their bordering trees. Company housing is at lower and upper right. Much of what is shown here has already been demolished.

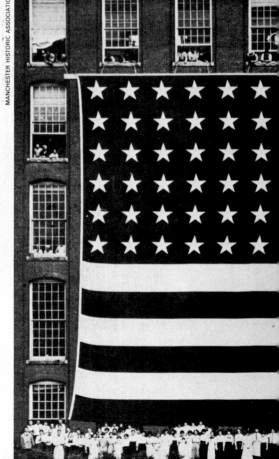

"Everybody took pride in working at the Amoskeag," one old employee recalls. It shows above. The photograph at right, taken in 1914 by a member of the employees' camera club, shows a sample of Amoskeag handiwork that measured 50 by 95 feet and was claimed to be the biggest flag ever made. It was ordered by someone in Chicago, for what purpose no one now knows; but according to local historians, all during its manufacture the flag never once touched the ground.

RANDOLPH LANGENBACH

RANDOLPH LANGENBACH, COURTESY SMITHSONIAN INSTITUTION

Amoskeag's handsome brick architecture was built to last and was marked by the quality of design in such ordinary things as a stairway.

and ninety feet wide, will slice through the mill yard, over the old canals, and all remaining cleared space will be covered over with enough asphalt to accommodate 2,500 cars. At this writing it appears that some of the large rectangular mills will survive, but even so they will be left stranded in a sea of automobiles. Plans like this "simple and sensible solution," as it has been called by advocates of urban renewal, have rarely if ever been the most creative solution; but increasingly they are becoming the "final solution" all over America.

At Manchester the alternative of making something of the Amoskeag mills, something inspired, such as a riverside cultural center (which might include a museum of New England's illustrious industrial history), or even something as plainly needed by the community as a branch of the state university, has been rejected for the short-term gain of parking space for a few modern industrial plants. The result will be a large contribution to the very chaos that is destroying the city's identity and sense of community. "Even with extensive improvements and upgrading, the millyard will never be an asset from an aesthetic point of view," the planners of Arthur

D. Little proclaimed; and that was that, even though it was abundant nonsense.

The modern American noncity with its freeway sprawl and its tasteless subdivision monotony is advancing rapidly across the land, and one readily identifiable community after another is being carved up, paved over, and obliterated.

At Manchester the nation has suffered just such a loss. Of course, by some people's standards the loss has been only a lot of old factories, and since the aesthetic value of anything is always a subjective matter, there is no easy way to refute this view. But that Amoskeag has long been a place of considerable historic importance, that the complex of mills, housing, and canals represented far more advanced urban planning and a more human environment than what it is being replaced by, and that the city of Manchester has lost an immensely fascinating and, to some, powerfully beautiful part of its heritage there is no doubt whatsoever. —*David G. McCullough*

The editors gratefully acknowledge the assistance of Mr. Randolph Langenbach, of Boston, who has been photographing and studying the Amoskeag mills for the past three years and is currently working on a book on the subject.

RANDOLPH LANGENBACH

"In its way Amoskeag was every bit as interesting as Williamsburg," says industrial historian William Pierson. Above: A sample of what is replacing Amoskeag. The sign at lower left is left over from a bitter local primary.

For a very long time it has been supposed that man could adjust himself to almost anything in the way of speed, noise, or financial outlay, just to get from one place to another in the least possible time. But the giant supersonic transport, the S.S.T., as it is known, is clearly something else again, and though President Nixon and others have said that the nation simply must have the superplane to maintain technological superiority in the skies, a growing number of Americans are questioning whether the plane itself is really necessary and, indeed, whether our national commitment to build it may be the beginning of a historic blunder of phenomenal proportions. In fact, Friends of the Earth, a new national conservation group with headquarters in New York, has singled out the S.S.T. as its first major target.

Promised by 1978, this superplane will carry three hundred passengers and cruise at eighteen hundred miles per hour at a stratospheric altitude of more than sixty thousand feet. The advance publicity indicates that it will be quiet enough inside, but outside it will lay down a continuous wave of sonic boom throughout the entire length of its flight. The total width of one S.S.T.'s wake of noise will be approximately fifty miles. For anyone caught in its path, the loudness of the sonic blast will be about equivalent to having a Boeing 707 roar three hundred feet over your living room, but the boom will come all at once and without warning, since the full impact of it is felt before the plane is seen or heard.

Yet the Air Force has called the boom "the sound of progress," just as early industrial air polluters announced that "smoke means jobs." The Boeing Com-

PHOTOGRAPH BY EMMA LANDAU

pany, manufacturer of the S.S.T. airframe, has described the boom as the sound of the twentieth century. And Major General Jewell C. Maxwell, the Federal Aviation Administration's former director for S.S.T. development, once predicted that people could learn to live with the boom—and maybe even love it.

Since President Kennedy first advocated the plane's development in 1963, the U.S. government has clearly committed itself to footing the bill for 78 per cent of a 1.65-billion-dollar research and development program. At the request of the Nixon administration Congress authorized eighty-five million dollars in new funds for the program this fiscal year and at the same time cut much-needed funds for urban mass transportation grants. Some economists predict that another three billion dollars will be spent before the first commercial S.S.T.'s are in the air.

Once in production, a single S.S.T. will cost about forty million dollars. An F.A.A. fact sheet projects a five-hundred-plane program by 1990, which means that the United States anticipates twenty billion dollars in sales, or more than enough to recoup its investment. Furthermore, twelve of those billions are anticipated from sales to foreign carriers. "However," the F.A.A. warns ominously, "if the U.S. S.S.T. is not built, U.S. flag carriers would buy more Concordes [the smaller Anglo-French supersonic jet already flight tested] and a total unfavorable swing of about $16 billion in balance of trade would occur." General Maxwell put a different twist on the balance-of-payments situation. In a mood reminiscent of George F. Babbitt's speech to the Rotarians, the general advised a New York City audience that one

S.S.T. sold abroad could offset thousands of imported cases of Scotch or virtually hundreds of foreign-made automobiles. But the general had no comment on what effect this same S.S.T. might have on the outflow of U.S. gold as it whisks thousands of Americans—and their dollars—to vacations abroad.

It was last September that President Nixon announced flatly that the superplane was indeed going to be built. For fifty years, he said, the United States has led the world in air transport. "I want to continue to lead . . ." he added. "After listening to all these arguments, I am convinced technical problems will be solved." But some of the President's advisers are not so sure. Mr. Nixon's own appointees to a special S.S.T. panel generally took the position that the superplane was economically—and environmentally—unsound. Their report, secreted away in the U.S. Department of Transportation, was finally uncovered and made public by Representative Henry S. Reuss, Democrat from Wisconsin, who called the report a "resounding nonendorsement of the S.S.T."

The panel found, among other things, that "the effects of sonic boom are such as to be considered intolerable by a very high percentage of the people affected." It also warned that people living within thirteen miles of an S.S.T. airport would be subjected to unacceptable levels of noise. And panelist Hendrik S. Houthakker, a member of Mr. Nixon's Council of Economic Advisers, strongly challenged the advisability of going forward with the S.S.T. when budget needs for more down-to-earth programs were so great. "We do not believe," he wrote in a letter accusing the Transportation Department of distorting the panel's views in a draft report, "that our prestige

SUPERPLANE

abroad will be enhanced by a concentration on white elephants."

Yet the S.S.T. seems to have its own momentum, and Mr. Nixon is not the only President to be scooped up in its path. Lyndon Johnson also ignored the report of his own study group, which advised that "there is absolutely no justification for building this plane."

Since Mr. Nixon's inexplicable decision, the outcry against the S.S.T. has grown in volume. "The administration talks about saving money," said Senator J. W. Fulbright of Arkansas, "and then decides to allocate huge sums for this plane." Representative Bertram Podell of Brooklyn wondered publicly how the administration could "torpedo" the proposed urban mass-transit trust fund, yet subsidize a vehicle that will "allow us to cross the ocean in two hours so we may be stuck in traffic jams for three." But perhaps the most telling commentary to date was delivered by a Stanford University law professor, William F. Baxter, who observed in a recent issue of the *Stanford Law Review:*

Present governmental generosity toward the SST program is a discouraging comment on our sense of national priorities: It may soon be possible to fly from Watts to Harlem in two hours and to disrupt the lives of everyone in between.

Superplane enthusiasts discount the latter possibility. John Volpe, the U.S. Secretary of Transportation, has pledged that there will be no overland flights by S.S.T.'s until the sonic boom has been brought within "acceptable limits." But at this writing Volpe has yet to define what he means by acceptable limits. Moreover, there is no foreseeable technological solution to the sonic-boom problem. A National Academy of Sci-

ences committee reported after two years of study that "prospects for dramatic reduction in the intensities of sonic boom . . . are not readily apparent." It is the inevitable result of propelling a heavy object through the air at such a speed (faster than the typical air molecule travels) that the air in front of the object is thrust aside in a few millionths of a second instead of flowing around the plane in the usual manner. The result is a sudden shock wave, a hurtling wall of compressed air, and there seems no way to avoid it.

The second fallacy of the pro-S.S.T. argument is that supersonic flights will necessarily be restricted to over-water routes. Who, including Mr. Volpe, will enforce such a restriction when (and there is only a negligible "if") the carriers begin to complain that they are losing not only *their* shirts, but the taxpayers' as well? Many observers believe the superplane will be incapable of turning a profit *unless* it flies over land. And finally, there is the curious assumption that people on ships at sea, or on islands, will somehow suffer less from the boom simply because there are fewer of them. An S.S.T. flight across the North Atlantic would "boom" some four thousand persons, which, of course, in terms of numbers would be preferable to the ten million Americans who might expect to be boomed by a coast-to-coast flight.

A sampling of past sonic-boom incidents suggests what may be expected when the superplane begins upholding the nation's aeronautical superiority:

May, 1968: Fifty thousand dollars' worth of windows shattered—appropriately enough during graduation exercises at the U.S. Air Force Academy in Colorado Springs. Injured: fifteen persons. The culprit: an F-105 flying at an

altitude of five hundred feet.

August, 1967: Three persons killed in the collapse of a barn in Mauran, France. The culprit: a sonic boom of unknown origin.

August, 1966: In Canyon de Chelly National Monument, Arizona, eighty tons of rock loosened on ancient Indian cliff dwellings; many caves damaged irreparably. More damage recorded in the time since then. The culprit: Strategic Air Command supersonic bombers.

January, 1965: Gordon Bains, then director of the S.S.T. program, is at White Sands Missile Range explaining to reporters that persons who claimed their property was damaged by sonic booms often were victims of their own imaginations. "I believe," he is saying, "that there's a great deal of psychology in this." Suddenly, five hundred feet overhead, an F-104 punctures the sound barrier. Two plate-glass windows blow out, cancelling Bains's banter.

But Professor Baxter of Stanford may have come even closer to the representative situation when he observed:

All the cracked $5 windowpanes, all the dinner dishes dropped on kitchen floors as a consequence of startled reactions, all the millions of hours of sleep lost while comforting frightened children, the razor-nicked chins, the interrupted concerts, the hammered thumbs, the crest-fallen cakes and omelets— all these will produce not litigation but at most a silent curse at the industry, at the FAA, or at a society that seems to many to have confused technology with civilization.

By some accounts the damage claims against the industry may run to two million dollars *a day* in the United States alone. And there will also be the as yet immeasurable, unlitigable effects upon man himself, be he ever so adaptable.

FIELD NOTES
By ELIZABETH N. LAYNE

A VISION ON THE HUDSON

"Sailing is like dancing, see, and I love to dance." The boat that Captain Allan Aunapu likes most to dance with is the *Clearwater* (above)—the first Hudson River sloop built in this century.

The *Clearwater*'s ancestry goes back to the days when the Dutch traded on the Hudson in their flat-bottomed sloops. After the British took over in 1664 a blend of English and Dutch design to handle the river's fluky winds and mean currents produced the famed nineteenth-century Hudson River sloop—broad in the beam, high in the stern, with an enormous mainsail. The boats averaged sixty to ninety feet in length and had masts over a hundred feet tall. At one time as many as eight hundred carried passengers and cargo between Albany and Manhattan. But steam—locomotives as well as boats—began to take over along the Hudson Valley in the early 1800's, and by the end of the century the sloops were gone. With steam came industry, large centers of population, and pollution. Today the river is a receptacle for more than 200,-000,000 gallons of raw sewage a day.

Four years ago a number of Hudson Valley residents, including folk singer Pete Seeger, decided that a return of the old sloop might help spark a sense of pride in the river and its heritage. They formed the Hudson River Sloop Restoration, Inc., and raised $175,000 to have the Gamage Shipyard in Maine build a seventy-six-foot replica, which they christened *Clearwater*. Last summer she sailed the river with a cargo of singers, including Seeger, and put on seven festivals with a message—care about your river and help clean it up. At the sloop's helm was twenty-eight-year-old Captain Aunapu, who though no musician, can be decidedly lyrical when talking about the *Clearwater* on the Hudson: "When you're running with a good wind up the river with that sixty-six-foot boom swung out over the water and maybe a full moon hanging off the end, or you're sailing through the Highlands and you have to tack right up close to the brow of the land and the wind comes down hard from between the mountains, you're dancing, dancing with the wind and the tides and the land in the most magnificent machine man ever invented. We want always to keep her under sail, never turn on her engine. We don't want people to look up and just see a mast being pushed through the water; we want their eyes to light up with a vision of what a beautiful part of his environment man can be."

This spring the *Clearwater* is sailing south to Washington, D. C., where she will lend her special grace to the national environmental teach-in on April 22.

"We get richer and richer in filthier and filthier communities until we reach a final state of affluent misery—Croesus on a garbage heap."
—John W. Gardner, head of the Urban Coalition.

QUIET PLEASE

Overexposure to excessive noise is the major cause of hearing loss in America. Nearly everyone, in fact, has lost hearing ability without realizing it. Power-driven appliances have made American homes the noisiest on earth, and "relaxing quietly at home" is fast becoming a thing of the past, for people never do get accustomed to noise. According to medical evidence, instinctive reaction to loud noise is fear

TYPICAL SOURCE	NOISE LEVELS*
	*decibels***
whisper	20
conversation	50
human annoyance threshold	50–60
window air conditioner	60
electric blender	70
hearing damage begins if prolonged	85
rush hour traffic	90
heavy construction	110
human pain threshold	120
rock music	up to 120
pneumatic riveter	125
jet takeoff	150

*at distances at which people are commonly exposed

**loudness increases ten times with each ten-decibel increase

and an impulse to escape. The heartbeat increases, arteries constrict, pupils dilate. One prominent scientist asserts that violent noise may even harm unborn babies.

Out on the street things are worse still. Air compressors, pile drivers, jackhammers, sirens, traffic, all add up to a noise level known to destroy hearing cells at prolonged exposure. "The saving quality heretofore," says one report, "has been that community noise has been a short-term exposure . . . as the power use of both home and street increases, steps must be taken to limit the noise output."

Down on the farm there is again less and less quiet. A recent government study reported that 90 per cent of fifty-eight new farm tractors tested made enough noise to be considered unsafe when the operator was subjected to it for a normal working day. And 65 per cent of such farm equipment as corn pickers, combines, and beet pullers exceeded recommended noise levels.

The Selective Service says that loud music is apparently to blame for the partial deafness that causes many draftees to be rejected. But it took the outrage of jet engine noise and the promise of a supersonic transport plane (see page 114) to finally stir people to action. In Inglewood, California, near Los Angeles Airport, where the din of air traffic has been described by one victim as "the equivalent of thirty Niagara Falls," two schools were closed because jets made teaching impossible. Near Kennedy Airport, on Long Island, one million people live within a zone of "unacceptable annoyance," as the F.A.A. describes it. Recently such besieged communities from twenty-three states formed NOISE, a Washington-based lobby.

Only in December did the F.A.A. begin to quiet the airways by setting regulations for the new jumbo jets. But the enormous new Boeing 747 is exempt, and not until 1971 are controls expected for jets now in operation. The only significant federal action has been in setting limits for industrial noise levels. Although authorization for such action has existed since 1935, nothing was done until 1969. Even then, the original proposal was compromised under pressure from such high-noise industries as textile manufacturing and set at ninety decibels, five more than experts consider safe (see chart).

Unlike most pollution problems, it is relatively easy to do something about noise levels. The technology is available and in many instances costs little. All the public has to do is . . . make some noise about it.

COUNTDOWN FOR POLAR BEARS

For the past few years light planes, boats, and snowmobiles have been taking hunters to the polar ice cap in such numbers that the polar bear may be threatened with extinction. The animal is being killed as never before. Even with strict regulation, the annual kill in Alaska (about four hundred) has more than tripled in twenty years and brings to the Alaskan economy over $600,000 a year. Of the five interpolar countries— Canada, United States, Norway, Denmark (Greenland), U.S.S.R.—only Russia fully protects the polar bear. In Norway a hunter can trap bears by

setting a baited gun. This often means cubs are left to die after the sow has taken the bait and been shot. With a snowmobile, a whole string of such traps can easily be maintained. The snowmobile has also become standard equipment for Eskimos and Indians in Canada, where by far the greatest number of bears are killed—six hundred a year.

In 1968 an international "Polar Bear Group" was formed under the auspices of the International Union for the Conservation of Nature and Natural Resources (I.U.C.N.) to study the bear's migration patterns, population, and ability to withstand arctic conditions. But unfortunately polar bear tracking and counting devices are still in their infancy. The current technique of state and federal teams in Alaska begins with finding the bear, using a ski-equipped light plane and a helicopter. Twenty minutes after the animal has been tranquilized with a dart gun fired from the helicopter, he is turned loose with a tag in each ear, an experimental collar about his neck, and big purple numbers on his flank to warn off hunters. He will also have been weighed by being dangled in a net from the helicopter, and he will have had one small tooth removed. (Like the rings of a tree, a tooth cross section will show his age.) Preliminary evidence from four hundred polar bears tagged during the past three springs indicates that the bear is not circumpolar, as was thought, and that there may be separate regional races. If true, this would mean each interpolar country could manage its own bear population.

The polar bear is large (up to a length of nine feet and a weight of one thousand pounds) and carnivorous (primarily seals), and he wanders over the ice drift

some twenty to forty miles a day in search of food. In fact, the bears never go to land except to have their young, and fewer and fewer of them are doing even that. They are tough animals to study. The best hope for successful tracking of the polar bear lies in electronic transmission—a radio transmitter on the bear's collar that will send a beep to an earth-circling Nimbus satellite. A transmitter and battery able to operate at 50 degrees below zero and to withstand frequent plunges into icy waters is being developed, and by 1971 polar bears will doubtless be tracked by satellite. But a simple counting mechanism is also badly needed. Population estimates vary widely—from ten to twenty thousand. The Alaskan teams are currently experimenting with airborne infrared scanning devices—the trick being to distinguish among the radiation thrown off by seals, bears, and arctic foxes.

James Brooks, who heads the federal government's team in Alaska, is worried that the enormous increase in human population there, brought on by the oil strike, will mean far too many dead bears. "The American kill is already at maximum safe levels," he says. Meanwhile, two of this country's most prestigious hunting groups, the Boone and Crockett Club and the National Rifle Association, have at least removed the polar bear from their trophy list.

It has been thirty-nine years since Rollin Kirby's cartoon, "The Public Enemy," appeared in the old New York World.

Letters to the Editor

CONSERVATION

Sir: . . . You told precisely the story that the National Audubon Society has been preaching: that conservation is no less than the battle to keep our planet livable and its environment worth living in. Articles like yours can help alert America, and conservation organizations like ours can help point the way for citizen action.

As a native Kentuckian, I was particularly interested in your story on my old friend and former student Harry Caudill and his fight to curb strip mining and to save the beautiful Red River Gorge—two fights in which the National Audubon Society and its Kentucky chapters have been deeply involved.

Elvis J. Stahr
President, National Audubon Society

Sir: I am an enthusiastic reader of AMERICAN HERITAGE magazine and read each issue from cover to cover.

Also I am a conservationist and support all efforts to preserve our environment in a livable condition and to correct the pollution of air, water, and land while still carrying out the necessary operations for life.

In your December, 1969, issue you depict a logging scene in your second full page spread which I would guess was in the redwood region, although it could easily be Douglas fir, ponderosa pine, or other species. The implication is that this is despoiling our land and forests, while in fact it is as much of a harvesting scene as a cornfield after picking.

Modern forest management has found that clear cutting is desirable to get the maximum forest reproduction in most coniferous species. In a few years the scene you show will be a beautiful stand of young trees. In seventy to eighty years it will be ready to harvest, if this is redwood, and the yield will surpass the crop just harvested.

This type of timber cropping must not be confused with the cutting of the very old redwood groves which occur on the valley floors. Most of the old groves are now in parks. If we are to have lumber for houses it must be grown and harvested.

I am irked by the confusing of timber harvesting with resource despoliation, and it has been frequently done in articles dealing with conservation problems. Timber is a renewable crop which is necessary for our needs.

O. W. Frost
Consultant
Wood Products and Processes
Grand Marais, Minnesota

Sir: There are not enough words available to praise AMERICAN HERITAGE magazine. As a charter subscriber, devoted supporter, and unofficial salesman for many years, I have been impressed that the quality of "our" magazine continues to move up while others decline. . . . How do I express adequate congratulations for your section on conservation and environmental issues?

Looking at the 1970's as the "environmental decade," the new section takes on a particular significance. Continued high quality articles such as those in the December, 1969, issue will contribute to the public's awareness of the environmental problems we face as a nation. Public understanding of the connection between America's heritage and its natural endowments is imperative if we are to save both for future generations.

John P. Saylor
Member of Congress
Pennsylvania, 22nd District

CATASTROPHE BY THE NUMBERS

Sir: A much stronger word than Congratulations is needed to express my admiration and gratitude for your publishing Charlton Ogburn's article "Catastrophe by the Numbers" (December, 1969). It is most lucid and courageous. That it should appear first in AMERICAN HERITAGE is indeed a magnificent testimony to your genuine concern not only for our country's heritage but for its future.

It is inevitable that some will remonstrate—those who are a part of that all too large a group who prefer the pleasant world of fantasy to the harsh world of reality. Others, thanks to you, will for the first time be enabled to see the horrors of overpopulation as an American problem. For too long our simplistic concern for the hungry masses of India has blinded us to the crisis in our own back yard.

The Reverend Canon Don C. Shaw
Chairman, First National Congress on Optimum Population and Environment
Chicago, Illinois

Sir: . . . I feel Charlton Ogburn's statements about Robert Kennedy's reproductive prowess were erroneous as well as in poor taste. If the more than 214,000,000 descendants of the Robert Kennedys inherited their wealth, wit, wisdom, and dedication, then I say the world owes the Kennedys a debt of gratitude. Someone once said to me she hoped Ethel had twenty children. I was appalled at the thought until she explained that as far as she was concerned one of the obligations of the rich is to have as many children as they can. It makes a lot of sense. The world could only improve if the rich were to have as many children as possible while the poor were attempting to "control themselves."

If I feel I can afford three, four, or more children, and as long as I don't become a burden on the nation, then how dare anyone tell me to stop after one or two? On the other hand, if this insane government of ours would *dis*courage the poor by refusing welfare to anyone with more than two children, I guarantee a drastic drop in the birth rate as well as welfare costs.

Thank God I won't live to see the chaos Mr. Ogburn describes. . . .

Rita M. Veneziani
Beltsville, Maryland

Sir: . . . I have grave doubt of the appropriateness in a magazine of history of a section on conservation. I have no doubt of the inappropriateness of certain language in Mr. Ogburn's article.

I refer to the language at page 116, "Congress, no longer palsied before native obscurantism or the medieval theology of the Vatican, has—admirably—appropriated substantial funds for rereach into human reproduction and for the dissemination of information on contraceptive techniques."

Also the statement at page 117, that "The Vatican has changed its mind in the past, and can and must change it again."

The unflattering and controversial references to the late Senator Robert Kennedy in this article also seem to me to be highly inappropriate.

Porter Risley
El Paso, Texas

JUSTICE TO FIRST INHABITANTS

Sir: In Alaska today sixty thousand Indians, Eskimos, and Aleuts are fighting peacefully to protect their lands from expropriation by the state of Alaska. Their struggle ranks in historical importance with the great Indian wars of the West a century ago. Some time in 1970 Congress is expected to enact legislation to settle Alaskan native land claims, and the reasonable demands of these claims offer the United States a priceless opportunity to do justice to its first inhabitants, whose treatment in the past reflects little glory on our nation. As far as justice is concerned, it is all on the side of the natives.

.They have conclusive legal and moral claims to most of Alaska's 375,000,000 acres. They have not sold their land, nor ceded it by treaty, nor lost it in war, and were generally secure in the possession of their land until the Statehood Act of 1958. At that time Congress granted Alaska the right to select 103,000,000 acres of land from the public domain. To protect native land rights against the new state, Congress stipulated that "the state and its people do agree and declare that they forever disclaim all right and title . . . to any lands or other property (including fishing rights) the right or title to which may be held by any Indians, Eskimos, or Aleuts." Despite this clear statement, the state has moved to take lands claimed by the natives, lands that are essential to their survival. Today's oil boom in Alaska threatens to accelerate greatly the dispossessing of the natives. The Atlantic Richfield oil strike at Prudhoe Bay and the $900,000,000

sale of oil exploration rights on a portion of the North Slope in September, 1969, are on lands taken by the state from the Eskimos.

The Indians, Eskimos, and Aleuts are among the few hunting and fishing societies remaining in the world today. They live in delicate balance with the land. At this moment in our history, when thinking Americans are growing increasingly alarmed at the destruction by man of man's environment, we can learn a lesson from the natives of Alaska that can help us preserve the land we live on for ourselves and future generations.

Concern for the property rights of America's aboriginal peoples has been a central feature of our public land policy from the earliest days of our government. A proclamation of the congress of the Confederation in 1783 and the ordinance for the Northwest Territory of 1787 establish the rule that aboriginal occupancy creates a property right that the United States alone has the power to extinguish.

In 1823 Chief Justice John Marshall, in the case of *Johnson v. M'Intosh*, first announced what has endured to the present day as the cornerstone of judicial recognition of the land rights of American Indians. America's original inhabitants are, he stated, "the rightful occupants of the soil with legal as well as just claims to retain possession of it." In the Organic Act of 1884 establishing territorial government in Alaska, Congress confirmed the natives' right to the land and pledged future legislation to convey title to them. For eighty-six years it has postponed action on this promise.

Despite all these legal commitments the Department of the Interior's Bureau of Land Management over the past decade has granted the state title to 6,000,000 acres of land and tentatively approved the transfer of another 12,000,000 acres. In response to native appeals Secretary of the Interior Stewart L. Udall in 1966 imposed a freeze on the transfer of additional lands and halted the issuance of new oil and gas leases on the public domain until Congress could make a disposition of native claims.

As a test case the then governor of Alaska, Walter J. Hickel, filed suit against Secretary Udall to compel him to grant to the state the lands of the Indian village of Nenana. The U.S. Court

of Appeals for the ninth district is now considering the case.

When Governor Hickel appeared at Senate confirmation hearings on his appointment by President Nixon to succeed Mr. Udall as Secretary of the Interior, Senator Henry M. Jackson obtained from him a promise that the land freeze would remain in effect until the Ninety-first Congress adjourns. Secretary Hickel has indicated that unless Congress acts by the end of 1970 he will resume the transfer of native lands to the state.

The Alaska Federation of Natives—representing the state's three aboriginal ethnic groups—has proposed in a bill now before Congress a fair and moderate compromise of land claims. Its proposal asks that title to 40,000,000 acres be apportioned among the many villages. This is roughly 10 per cent of the land to which they are entitled. In return for the extinguishment of their claims to more than 300,000,000 acres of other land, worth tens of billions of dollars, the natives ask only for cash compensation in the amount of $500,000,000 (about $1.50 an acre) and a 2 per cent royalty on minerals. The monetary settlement would not be paid to individuals but rather to native-owned village, regional, and statewide development corporations, so that the money would go to launch essential self-help programs in health, education, housing, employment, and economic growth. In contrast, the federal government has offered $500,000,000, no royalty, and 12,000,000 acres of land, *without* mineral rights.

The settlement proposed by the Alaska Federation of Natives is just, reasonable, and humane. With a secure land base and sufficient capital the natives would be able to assure rational and coherent development of their natural resources without disrupting the ecology of the land—a land they have never despoiled. Justice demands that Congress and the American people do not deny them the chance they deserve.

Arthur J. Goldberg

Arthur J. Goldberg, former Supreme Court Justice and U.S. ambassador to the United Nations, is serving as general counsel for the Alaska Federation of Natives as a public service. Associated with him in this effort are former Attorney General Ramsey Clark and former U.S. Senator Thomas Kuchel.—Ed.

SAM ORKIN'S NAVY

The curious sight above takes us back to the recruiting and Liberty Bond drives of World War I, to a time when the engines of war were as popular as "preparedness" itself. These gentlemen have just launched a miraculous working model of the then-powerful dreadnought U.S.S. *Pennsylvania*. They belong to no military-industrial complex except the toy business, and they plan to do their patriotic bit by exhibiting their stuff in stores all over the country.

This fine model was the brain child of Samuel Orkin, who appears second from right, in glasses, beaming with pride. Mr. Orkin, born in Kiev, Russia, in 1891, immigrated with his family to Boston when he was seven, managed to get through two years of the Boston Mechanics High School, and then had to go to work in the family jewelry business. Had he only been able to get more education, it seems likely that he might have become a very notable man; his achievements without it are as astounding as his luck was bad. After his Navy-sponsored tours of stores (one of whose ads appears in part below), he started a toy-boat factory. It foundered in the Depression. He started another, which expired in the subsequent recession. He imported toys; he sold liquor wholesale (in partnership with a son of Francis X. Bushman, the movie actor); he became a tool-and-die maker in World War II for Lockheed; and he invented a method for printing colored pictures on plastic. At the moment, Sam Orkin, now seventy-eight, is still going strong and has invented a means of reproducing paintings in rhinestones, an unlikely and somewhat blinding art form which may yet prove to have a market. Mr. Orkin's daughter Ruth, a noted New York photographer, brought us this picture as a curiosity and told us that she remembers seeing the boat long ago when she was a little girl. Lightning flashed between the telegraph towers, guns went off, and smoke poured out of the stacks while tiny sailors raced up and down the decks on an endless chain. "Father could make anything," says Miss Orkin; the only trouble was that he was terrible when it came to helping her with homework.